# Teacup Yorkies or Toy Yorkies

## The Ultimate Teacup Yorkie Dog Manual

What you need to know before you buy a Teacup Yorkie.

by

George Hoppendale

and

Asia Moore

ALL RIGHTS RESERVED. This book contains material protected under International and Federal Copyright Laws and Treaties.

Any unauthorized reprint or use of this material is strictly prohibited. No part of this book may be reproduced or transmitted in any form or by any means, electronic, mechanical or otherwise, including photocopying or recording, or by any information storage and retrieval system without express written permission from the author.

Copyrighted © 2014
Author: George Hoppendale
Author: Asia Moore - Ask a Dog Whisperer
K-9SuperHeroesDogWhispering.com

Published by: IMB Publishing

Table of Contents

# Table of Contents

*Table of Contents* ................................................................. 3
*About the Authors* ............................................................... 8
*Chapter 1: Introduction* ....................................................... 9
*Chapter 2: The Teacup Yorkie* ........................................... 10
    1. Yorkshire Terrier ......................................................... 10
    2. History/Origin of the Teacup Yorkie ........................... 13
    3. Teacup Yorkie Secrets ................................................ 13
    4. Famous Movie Dogs ................................................... 15
    5. Famous War Dog Story ............................................... 15
    6. Every Dog ................................................................... 20
*Chapter 3: Teacupism* ......................................................... 23
    Severe Health Problems .................................................. 26
*Chapter 4: Breeding* ............................................................ 30
    1. Father of the Breed ..................................................... 31
    2. Huddersfield Ben ........................................................ 31
    3. In North America ........................................................ 32
    4. Biewer Yorkie .............................................................. 33
    5. Locating a Reputable Breeder ...................................... 33
    6. Meet the Parents ........................................................ 34
    7. Questions to Ask a Breeder ......................................... 34
*Chapter 5: Vital Statistics* .................................................... 39
    1. Country of Origin ........................................................ 39
    2. Litter Size ................................................................... 39
    3. Height and Weight ...................................................... 39
    4. Temperature & Heart Rate ......................................... 40
    5. Lifespan ...................................................................... 40
    6. Intelligence ................................................................ 40
    7. Living Conditions ........................................................ 41
*Chapter 6: Temperament* .................................................... 44
    1. Behavior With Children and Pets ................................ 46
    2. Toy Dogs Can Be Prey ................................................. 46

## Table of Contents

    3. Is This Dog an Escape Artist? ............................................................. 47

*Chapter 7: Before You Buy* .......................................................................... 48
    1. Pros of Yorkie Ownership ................................................................... 49
    2. Cons of Yorkie Ownership .................................................................. 49

*Chapter 8: Choosing the Right Dog* ............................................................. 51
    1. Where to Purchase a US Puppy .......................................................... 51
    2. Where to Purchase a UK Puppy .......................................................... 51
    3. Average Prices for Puppies ................................................................. 51
    4. Avoiding Puppy Mills or Farms ........................................................... 52
    5. How to Choose the Right Puppy ......................................................... 54
    6. How to Check If a Puppy is Healthy ................................................... 58
    7. One Teacup Yorkie, or Two? ................................................................ 59
    8. Best Age to Purchase a Puppy ............................................................ 61
    9. Should I Get a Male or Female? .......................................................... 62
    10. The Teacup Yorkie Shopping List ...................................................... 63
    11. Puppy Proofing Your Home ............................................................... 65
    12. Puppy Hazard Home Inspection ....................................................... 68
    13. First Weeks With Your Puppy ............................................................ 68
    14. Common Mistakes to Avoid ............................................................... 73
    15. Bonding With Your Dog ..................................................................... 77

*Chapter 9: Health Problems* ........................................................................ 80
    1. Common Issues .................................................................................... 80
    2. Congenital Defects ............................................................................... 81
    3. Fragility .................................................................................................. 90
    4. Allergies ................................................................................................. 92

*Chapter 10: Daily Feeding and Care* ........................................................... 94
    1. Feeding Puppies ................................................................................... 94
    2. Feeding Adults ...................................................................................... 94
    3. Treats ..................................................................................................... 95
    4. Treats to Avoid ...................................................................................... 96
    5. Healthy Treats ....................................................................................... 98
    6. Choosing the Right Food ..................................................................... 99
    7. The Raw Diet ...................................................................................... 103
    8. The Dehydrated Diet ......................................................................... 105
    9. The Kibble Diet ................................................................................... 106
    10. The Right Bowl ................................................................................. 106

## Table of Contents

    11. Exercise .................................................................. 108
    12. Playtime ................................................................. 108
    13. Daily Grooming ...................................................... 109
    14. Safe Traveling ........................................................ 109

*Chapter 11: House Training* ............................................ 115
    1. Human Training ....................................................... 115
    2. Bell Training ............................................................. 117
    3. Kennel Training ........................................................ 118
    4. Exercise Pen Training ............................................... 119
    5. Puppy Apartment™ Training ................................... 120
    6. Free Training ........................................................... 122
    7. Mistakes Happen ..................................................... 123
    8. Electronic Training Devices ...................................... 124

*Chapter 12: Medical Care & Safety* ................................. 128
    1. Choosing a Veterinarian ........................................... 128
    2. Neutering and Spaying ............................................ 129
    3. Why Vaccinate a Puppy? .......................................... 133
    4. Other Diseases and Viruses ..................................... 137
    5. Additional Vaccinations ........................................... 145
    6. When Is a Puppy Vaccinated? .................................. 145
    7. De-Worming ............................................................ 146
    8. Special Care When Pregnant ................................... 146
    9. Licensing ................................................................. 148
    10. Pet Insurance ........................................................ 148
    11. Identifying and Finding Lost Dogs .......................... 152
    12. Yearly Cost of Ownership ...................................... 155

*Chapter 13: Coat Colors and Types* ................................ 159
    1. Style ........................................................................ 159
    2. Body Color .............................................................. 159
    3. Puppy Coats ............................................................ 160
    4. Adult Coats ............................................................. 162
    5. Coat Types & Colors ................................................ 162
    6. Tail Docking ............................................................ 167
    7. Defining Features ................................................... 168

*Chapter 14: Grooming* ................................................... 169
    1. Bath Time ............................................................... 170

## Table of Contents

- 2. Ear Care ... 173
- 3. Eye Care ... 173
- 4. Nail Care ... 174
- 5. Dental Care ... 175
- 6. Skin Care ... 180
- 7. Pest Control ... 180
- 8. Brushing and Combing ... 181
- 9. Equipment Required ... 181
- 10. Products ... 183
- 11. Professional Grooming ... 188

*Chapter 15: Socializing* ... *190*
- 1. With Other Dogs and Pets ... 190
- 2. With Other People ... 192
- 3. Within Different Environments ... 193
- 4. Loud Noises ... 194

*Chapter 16: Training* ... *196*
- 1. Trainability ... 196
- 2. Puppy Training Basics ... 197
- 3. Beginner Leash Lesson ... 199
- 4. Surviving Adolescence ... 201
- 5. Releasing Energy ... 203
- 6. The Unruly Adolescent ... 204
- 7. Rewarding Unwanted Behavior ... 205
- 8. Back to Basics ... 207
- 9. Sit and More Sit ... 207
- 10. Giving Up is Not an Option ... 209
- 11. Re-visit Basic First Commands ... 212
- 12. Hand Signals ... 215
- 13. Simple Tricks ... 218
- 14. Adult Training ... 220
- 15. Behavioral Issues ... 222
- 16. Overheating ... 223

*Chapter 17: Poisonous Foods & Plants* ... *224*
- 1. Poisonous Foods ... 224
- 2. Poisonous Household Plants ... 230
- 3. Poison Proof Your Home ... 235

## Table of Contents

- 4. Garden Plants ............................................................................ 236
- 5. Why Does My Dog Eat Grass? ................................................. 236
- 6. Animal Poison Control Centre ................................................. 237

*Chapter 18: Caring for Aging Dogs* .................................................... *238*
- 1. What to Be Aware Of ................................................................ 238
- 2. How to Make Them Comfortable ............................................ 241
- 3. What is Euthanasia? ................................................................. 244
- 4. When to Help a Dog Transition ............................................... 245
- 5. Grieving a Lost Pet .................................................................... 246
- 6. The Rainbow Bridge Poem ....................................................... 248
- 7. Memorials .................................................................................. 249

*Chapter 19: Rescue Organizations* ..................................................... *251*
- 1. Shelters ...................................................................................... 251
- 2. Online Resources ...................................................................... 251
- 3. Canine Clubs and Breeders ...................................................... 251

*Chapter 20: Resources & References* .................................................. *252*
- 1. Poison Control .......................................................................... 252
- 2. Breeders, Registries & Rescues ................................................ 252
- 3. Equipment, Supplies & Services .............................................. 252
- 4. Memorials .................................................................................. 253

## About the Authors

**George Hoppendale** is an experienced writer and a true animal lover. He enjoys writing animal books and advising others how to take care of their animals to give them a happy home.

**Asia Moore** is an animal lover, professional Dog Whisperer, Cynologist and experienced Author, living on Vancouver Island, off the west coast of British Columbia, in Canada, who believes that all humans and dogs can live together in harmony.

She and her dog whispering team, which includes an 8-year-old Shih Tzu named Boris, teach dog psychology to humans, to help alleviate problem behaviors that arise through misunderstandings between humans and their canine counterparts so that everyone can live a happy and stress-free life together.

Visit Asia and her dog whispering team online at: K-9SuperHeroesDogWhispering.com

# Chapter 1: Introduction

It's important to gather as much information as possible before you take the plunge to share your home with a furry friend.

The Ultimate Teacup Yorkie Dog Manual will answer the questions you may have when researching this hybrid canine. If you are considering sharing your home with the active and intelligent Yorkshire Terrier, this Manual is for you.

Learn all about this purebred canine, including facts and secrets about both breeds, and how to care for every stage of the Teacup Yorkie's life.

This Manual contains all the information you need, including a section dedicated to "teacupism", choosing a breeder and finding the perfect puppy to how to care for an aging dog.

As well, you will learn about transitioning through house breaking, adolescence, daily care, health problems in inherent in the breed, feeding, grooming, training, first commands, basic hand signals and end of life, so that you can make an educated decision when deciding whether or not the intelligent and energetic Teacup Yorkie is the breed for you and your family.

As well, this manual contains valuable information, tips and tricks that can easily be applied to any breed of canine.

## Chapter 2: The Teacup Yorkie

The *"Teacup Yorkie"* is a very small, purebred Yorkshire Terrier, also called *"Toy Yorkie"*.

While the appearance and size of the Teacup Yorkie will largely depend upon the appearance and size of both parents, this will be a very small toy breed of dog.

The Teacup Yorkie hybrid can take on more of the physical appearance and traits of the Yorkshire Terrier parent or more of the physical appearance and traits of the Poodle parent.

When measured at the shoulder, the Teacup Yorkie will stand between 4 and 6 inches (10.16 and 15.24 centimeters) and weigh less than 4 pounds (less than 1.81 kilograms), depending on the size of both parents.

### 1. Yorkshire Terrier

Tough and tenacious, terriers are well known for bravely seizing the day and everything in it with much gusto and an excess of spirit.

These little working dogs were miniaturized from hounds to follow prey underground and hence, their name comes from the French word *"terre"*, which literally means *"earth"*.

## Chapter 2: The Teacup Yorkie

These small terriers were bred to kill vermin or drag them out of the ground, and this work required dogs to be small in size but large and fearless in spirit, so that they would tunnel with enthusiasm and confront opponents from foxes or badgers to dogs many times their size without a second thought.

While they were described as early as the 16th century as quarrelsome and snappy, terriers are endlessly entertaining, and for most people, it is difficult not to fall in love with their sheer lust for life.

The Yorkshire Terrier or *"Yorkie"* is a purebred toy breed of dog generally weighing 7 pounds (3.2 kilograms).

Although the Yorkie breed has it's true origins in Scotland, it was actually named after the location where the breed was developed by workers who travelled from Scotland to Yorkshire in northern England searching for work during the middle 19$^{th}$ century.

During the time of the Industrial Revolution, Scottish workers traveled north looking for work in coal mines, textile mills and factories, and settled in Yorkshire, England. When these workers travelled, they brought along with them a variety of small terriers, including the Clydesdale or Paisley Terrier who were much larger than today's smaller Yorkshire terrier.

The original ancestors of the modern Yorkie were dogs crossed with other types of terriers, such as the English Black and Tan Toy terrier, the Skye terrier, and the small Waterside terrier, which had a long, blue-grey coat.

These many mixes of terriers became the fore bearers of the breed now recognized as the Yorkshire terrier.

As a result of the human desire to breed ever smaller sized dogs, today the Yorkie is considered a toy sized companion breed.

## Chapter 2: The Teacup Yorkie

The American Kennel Club (AKC) and the United Kennel Club (UKC) both recognized the Yorkie as a purebred canine in 1885 and 1956 respectively.

This very popular companion dog has also played an instrumental part in the development of other breeds, including the Silky Terrier, or Australian Silky Terrier, which is a very close descendant of the Yorkshire Terrier, being very similar in coat color and look.

In North America, and throughout the world, the Yorkie remains one of the most popular small terrier breeds.

Statistics indicate that according to American Kennel Club registrations, the Yorkie continues to rank highly in popularity, holding the #6 position amongst 175 registered breeds in both 2012 and 2013.

During the 1970's Yorkies were the most popular breed of dog in British Kennel Club, reaching their peak in popularity in 1990. Today, the Yorkie is still listed as the 7$^{th}$ most popular breed in the United Kingdom.

Kennel Club weight standards for this breed have reduced significantly from what the original weight of a Yorkie used to be before the 1930's when the Yorkshire Terrier weighed between 15 and 30 pounds (6 and 13 kilograms).

Once the Yorkie breed left the workforce lifestyle behind, they quickly joined the ranks of European high society families where they became pampered companions to the idle rich as well as impressive show dogs.

Today, for show purposes, the Kennel Club weight standard for the Yorkshire Terrier breed is between 3 and 7 pounds (1 and 3.2 kilograms) and rather than being classed as working terriers, they are classed in the *"toy"* category.

*Chapter 2: The Teacup Yorkie*

## 2. History/Origin of the Teacup Yorkie

While determining true origin of a specific breed of canine is always met with a certain degree of controversy and many different theories about the true origin of a breed, since the Yorkshire Terrier has not been prized for their superior hunting abilities when eliminating vermin for a very long time, they have become a much smaller dog, registered with the American Kennel Club (ACK) as a toy variety of companion canine.

While the Teacup Yorkie will usually be a loving, affectionate and sweet natured dog inside the home, that will follow you everywhere, when not trained properly, this excited little companion, can be possessive of its guardian, and depending on the particular dog, the hunting heritage may take over when they get outside and see birds, rabbits, cats or rodents to chase.

The popularity of this already toy sized purebred canine has likely escalated in recent years due to their popularity with celebrities as they fit so conveniently inside those expensive designer handbags.

## 3. Teacup Yorkie Secrets

The name *"Teacup Yorkie"* is merely a descriptive term for a Yorkshire Terrier dog purported to be smaller than the accepted breed standard.

The Yorkshire Terrier was originally named the *"Scotch Terrier"*.

During the earliest history of the Yorkshire Terrier breed, this canine was used for a popular blood sport, called *"rat baiting"*, which involved placing many rats into a pit deep enough that they could not climb out, so that humans could place bets on how long it would take for a terrier placed in their midst to kill all the rats.

Although the UK implemented the *Cruelty to Animals Act* in 1835, this *Act* only prohibited the baiting of larger animals, such

## Chapter 2: The Teacup Yorkie

as the bear and the bull, which meant that ratting competitions became a very popular gambling sport, with rat pits in London numbering more than 70.

Thankfully, this blood sport was banned at the beginning of the 20<sup>th</sup> century.

While Yorkies are very popular throughout the world, they are especially popular in New York City where there is a high concentration of Yorkies.

Tricia Nixon's pet Yorkie, *"Pasha"*, lived in the White House during the Richard Nixon presidency.

A matchbox-sized Yorkie, named *"Sylvia"*, owned by Arthur Marples of Blackburn, England, enjoys fame for being the smallest dog in recorded history. Sylvia stood a tiny 2½ inches (6.35 centimetres) at the shoulder and weighed only 4 ounces (113 milligrams). She died in 1945 when she was just two years old.

Prior to 1995, a 5½-inch (13.97 centimetre) Yorkie named *"Thumbelina"*, held the Guinness World Record for smallest living dog.

The Yorkshire Terrier breed was first registered in the British Kennel Club studbook during the year 1874, and the first English breed club was formed 24 years later, in 1898.

1872 is the year attributed to the earliest record of a Yorkie having been born in the United States.

As a result of this breed's great favor with many Hollywood celebrities and wealthy women who carry them around as fashion statements, the intelligent Yorkshire Terrier is generally what comes to mind (next to the Chihuahua) when someone says, *"Purse Dog,"* as they've been carried around in fancy handbags or under celebrity armpits for many centuries.

*Chapter 2: The Teacup Yorkie*

A Yorkie named *"Ozzy"* became the most expensive Yorkie ever purchased when Ozzie Osbourne and his wife Sharon paid $10,000 (£5,884) at a 2011 auction to benefit those suffering from autism and Parkinson's disease.

## 4. Famous Movie Dogs

Audrey Hepburn's Yorkshire Terrier named *"Mr. Famous"* who starred with Audrey in the 1957 movie "Funny Face" assured America's love of this adorable little dog.

Then *"Hootie"* the Yorkshire Terrier starred in a famous horror movie called *"Urban Legend"* that featured a Yorkie drinking beer through a beer bong.

Many other movies, films and TV shows featured the adorable Yorkshire Terrier, including *"Daltry Calhoun"*, *"A Fish Called Wanda"*, *"High School Musical 2"*, *"Cats and Dogs"*, *"Green Acres"*, *"Groomer Has It"* and *"Lou Grant"*.

## 5. Famous War Dog Story

One of the most amazing *"war dog"* stories every told is about the invincible spirit of a tiny, 4-pound (1 kilogram) Teacup Yorkie named *"Smoky"*.

Tiny Smoky, a decorated canine World War II hero, who was nicknamed the "*Yorkie Doodle Dandy"* served alongside Corporal Wynne with the 26$^{th}$ Photo Reconnaissance Squadron in the 5th Air Force.

She was found in an abandoned foxhole in the New Guinea jungle in 1944, and then adopted by Corporal William Wynne of Cleveland, Ohio who purchased her from a GI for $6.44 (£3.79), which was the price needed to remain in the poker game, while he was serving with the 5th Air Force in the Pacific.

Tiny but tenacious little Smoky backpacked through the rest of

## Chapter 2: The Teacup Yorkie

the war as she accompanied Corporal Wynne on many combat flights in the Pacific where she had to withstand the high humidity and equatorial heat of the New Guinea jungle.

Despite not having access to veterinary care or a balanced dog food diet, she was never ill while she shared Corporal Wynne's C-rations, an occasional can of Spam and his tent.

She was a tough little dog who even ran over sharp coral for four months without developing any of the paw problems that plagued some larger war dogs.

The celebrated Smoky flew a total of twelve air/sea rescue and photo reconnaissance missions and during those flights, she spent long hours patiently hanging in a soldier's pack near machine guns that were used to fend off enemy fighters.

Little Smoky survived 150 air raids on New Guinea, a typhoon at Okinawa, parachuting out of a tree while wearing a parachute made just for her, for which she was awarded eight battle stars.

Smoky was also affectionately called the *"angel from a foxhole"* because her keen hearing saved Corporal Wynne's life when she warned him of incoming shells that were about to strike an LST (Landing Ship Tank transport ship).

Even in the middle of all the extreme noise on the ship deck, with booming and vibrating from anti-aircraft gunnery, Smoky was still able to hear the high pitched sound of the incoming shells in time to guide Corporal Wynne to escape the fire that hit eight other soldiers standing next to them.

Of course, Smoky was much more than an angel just for Corporal Wynne, because during moments of down time, she shared her indomitable spirit and joy of life with everyone around her.

She was a dog that was always working, learning new tricks and bringing smiles to many faces as she performed for the

## Chapter 2: The Teacup Yorkie

entertainment of troops with Special Services and in hospitals from Australia to Korea.

According to Corporal Wynne, Smoky taught the Corporal just as much as he taught her, while developing a performance repertoire well beyond that of any dog of her day.

*"Yank Down Under"* Magazine (a weekly magazine published by the United States military during World War II) named Smoky the *"Champion Mascot in the Southwest Pacific Area"* in 1944."

However, smart and entertaining little Smoky was so much more than a mascot because the tricks she learned enabled her to become a true war hero in her own right.

Smoky was instrumental in helping engineers build a crucial airfield at Lingayen Gulf, Luzon (an extension of the South China Sea in the Philippines), which was a crucial air base for Allied warplanes.

Early in the Luzon campaign, the Signal Corps needed to run a telegraph wire through a 70-foot-long (21 meter) pipe that was only 8 inches (200 millimeters) in diameter.

Smoky was a critical component in completing this plan as she displayed her original working terrier breeding of going into holes in the ground to kill vermin, by carrying a telegraph wire through the pipe.

The problem with the plan was that soil had sifted through the corrugated sections where the pipes were joined together, filling in as much as half of the pipe, which gave Smoky only about four inches (100 millimeters) of space to crawl through in some places.

Corporal Wynne himself told the story of Smoky's bravery and tenacity, when he and Smoky appeared on NBC-TV:

> *"I tied a string (tied to the wire) to Smoky's collar and ran to the other end of the culvert . . . (Smoky) made a few steps*

## Chapter 2: The Teacup Yorkie

*in and then ran back. 'Come, Smoky,' I said sharply, and she started through again. When she was about 10 feet in, the string caught up and she looked over her shoulder as much as to say 'what's holding us up there?' The string loosened from the snag and she came on again. By now the dust was rising from the shuffle of her paws as she crawled through the dirt and mold and I could no longer see her. I called and pleaded, not knowing for certain whether she was coming or not. At last, about 20 feet away, I saw two little amber eyes and heard a faint whimpering sound . . . at 15 feet away, she broke into a run. We were so happy at Smoky's success that we patted and praised her for a full five minutes."*

Smoky's brave work negated the need to move several hundred crewmen, who would have been needed to dig up the runway, and instead, kept many US fighters and reconnaissance planes operational.

Smoky's bravery and indomitable spirit kept many men out of danger by turning what would have been a dangerous three-day digging task for the men to place the wire, into a task that was completed by this amazing little dog in just minutes.

When Smoky and Corporal Wynne returned home to Cleveland after the war, the Cleveland Press featured them both in a front-page story.

This was the beginning of Smoky becoming a national sensation which saw her and Wynne, over the next ten years, travelling all over the world, including Hollywood, where she performed her many amazing tricks for her adoring fans, including walking a tightrope while blindfolded.

Stardom followed Smoky wherever she went and she was so popular that she and Wynne even had a children's show of their own, called *"Castles in the Air",* which of course featured Smoky's unbelievable tricks.

## Chapter 2: The Teacup Yorkie

After starring on the WKYC station, Wynne and Smoky went on to WNBK, where he hosted a popular Sunday morning television show called *"How to Train Your Dog,* with Bill Wynne and Smoky."

The talented Smoky entertained many millions during the late 1940's and early 1950's, when she appeared in 42 live television performances, amazing audiences without ever repeating a single trick.

After an amazing career and ten years of performing for millions of adoring fans, Smoky retired from the bright lights and became a family pet, entertaining Bill and Margie's nine children, rather than strangers.

Smoky was also credited with being the forerunner for therapy dogs because amidst all her other performances, she also spent a lot of time doing what she did best, by raising spirits at veterans' hospitals.

On February 21, 1957, Smoky died peacefully in her sleep at the approximate age of 14 years, at the Wynne's home in Parma Heights.

The amazing story of Smoky the War Dog didn't end here, though.

The local paper reported Smoky's death the next day and the family was still mourning when they received a call that would, after all these years, finally solve the mystery of how Smokey ended up in that foxhole.

A nurse at the Crile Veterans Hospital by the name of Grace Heidenreich, who had read Smoky's obituary, made a call to the Wynne's home and told Bill and his family, *"This may sound strange, but I lost a female Yorkshire Terrier at a USO show when I was serving at a field hospital in New Guinea in 1944."*

*Chapter 2: The Teacup Yorkie*

During 1944 there were only 92 Yorkshire Terrier puppies registered in the entire United States and even fewer in Australia where Grace Heidenreich had purchased her puppy.

This news made it pretty clear that the dog Heidenreich lost was the amazing, little Smoky, and even more amazing was that after all these years, ten thousand miles, and more than a decade later, Smoky's two best friends discovered that they were close neighbors who lived just two blocks from each other.

Wynne and his family laid Smoky to rest inside a World War II .30 Caliber Ammunition Box in the Cleveland Metro parks, Rocky River Reservation in Lakewood, Ohio.

Almost 50 years later, a bronze, life-size sculpture of Smoky, depicted sitting inside a GI helmet, on top of a two ton blue granite base was unveiled on Veterans Day, November 11, 2005 dedicated to *"Smoky, the Yorkie Doodle Dandy, and Dogs of All Wars."*

Another special monument, featuring a small photograph of Smoky, honors the amazing spirit of the Yorkshire Terrier with the words *"World War II's littlest soldier and most famous war dog"*. This monument proudly stands at the Eastlake Doggie Park in the eastern suburbs of Cleveland, Ohio.

## 6. Every Dog

Please understand that much of the content written in this book can be applied to EVERY dog, because when it comes right down to it, a dog is a dog no matter what size, shape, colour, price tag or fancy hybrid name we humans might attribute to them.

Every dog has a uniquely wonderful set of gifts to share with their human counterparts, if only us humans would listen.

## Chapter 2: The Teacup Yorkie

They "tell" us when they are unhappy, when they are bored, when they are under-exercised, yet often we do not pay attention, or we just think they are being badly behaved.

Many humans today are deciding to have dogs, instead of children, and then attempting to manipulate their dogs into being small (or large) fur children. This is having a seriously detrimental effect upon the health and behaviour of our canine companions.

In order to be the best guardians for our dogs, we humans need to have a better understanding of what our dogs need from us, rather than what we need from them, so that they can live in safety and harmony within our human environment.

Sadly, many of us humans are not well equipped to give our dogs what they really need and that is why there are so many homeless, abandoned and frustrated dogs.

As a professional dog whisperer who is challenged with the task of finding amicable solutions for canine/human relationships that have gone bad, once the humans understand what needs to be changed, almost every stressful canine/human relationship can be turned into a happy, forever after.

The sad part is that many humans are simply not willing to do the work and devote the time necessary to ensuring that their dog's needs are met.

Almost all canine problems are a direct result of ignorance or unwillingness on the part of the canine guardian to learn what the dog truly needs. Forget about the breed for the moment, because what the dog needs to be a happy and well-balanced family member has nothing to do with size, shape, colour or breed.

First and foremost, our dogs need to be respected for their unique canine qualities.

For millennia, dog has been considered *"Man's best friend"*, and in today's society, when we want to do the best by our canine companions and create a harmonious relationship, we humans need to spend more time receiving the proper training so that we humans can learn how Man can be dog's best friend.

A Teacup Yorkie is a dog and therefore can be "Man's best friend" providing that the human guardian gains the knowledge they need in order to create a happy environment for the dog.

That's the biggest *"secret"* because if the human treats the dog well and understands what the dog needs, the dog will be happy and the owner will be happy. This is a universal truth that applies to any dog, whether a Teacup Yorkie or any other breed.

For example, it is not possible to write a book specifically about *"How to train a Teacup Yorkie"* or specifically about what "The first few days with your Teacup Yorkie" will entail, etc., as while basic training techniques apply to every dog, every dog and every human/dog relationship will be unique.

For this reason, when referring to daily feeding, care, house training, behavioural training, socializing, etc., these chapters are not written to apply specifically to the Teacup Yorkie breed, as this information can be applied equally successfully to any dog.

What we humans need to remember is that it is absolutely true that *"With the proper training, Man can learn to be dog's best friend."*

## Chapter 3: Teacupism

> ### *What you need to know before you buy a Teacup dog!*

The word *"teacup"* is often used to describe abnormally small, or *"teacup"* sized dogs, such as the Yorkie.

Usually dogs described as "teacup" sized are already toy sized breeds, and when a breeder adds the word "teacup" to the description of the dogs they are breeding, they are inferring that their dogs are ultra small sized.

*"Teacup"* sized dogs are also a current craze that comes with a very high price tag, therefore, despite the health risks associated to the dogs involved, it is no small wonder that you will easily be able to find numerous unscrupulous breeders eagerly jumping on this money-making bandwagon.

As a general rule, any adult dog weighing less than 4 pounds is considered to be "teacup" sized.

Many canine guardians may not be aware of the considerable health issues and risks which can be associated with owning such a small sized dog, including heart disease, luxating patella (floating kneecaps), hydrocephaly (water on the brain), hypoglycemia (low blood sugar), open fontanels (soft spots on the head) and seizures.

All of these health problems occur simply because creating such tiny dogs usually means that they are inbred, where the smallest, least healthy, "runt" of the litter will be bred to the smallest, least healthy or "runt" of another litter until the puppies being born become so small that they will be fortunate to survive at all.

*Breeding "teacup" sized dogs* is not encouraged by responsible

## Chapter 3: Teacupism

breeders who consider this to be a highly controversial practice because it creates weak, unstable dogs that can suffer from many health problems throughout their life, including a considerably shortened lifespan.

Perhaps these miniaturized versions of already very small dogs, which are considerably smaller than any officially recognized breed, are so popular because it is a sign of the times we live in, where we humans have fallen in love with the idea of increasingly shrinking technology, such as cell phones, computers and printers, and this has trend as also transitioned over to our dogs.

Perhaps it's time we humans took a closer look at what the ultra small fad is creating in the canine world because once we have all the facts, we can choose not be part of a practice that has far reaching consequences. For instance, there are at least four pressing and compelling reasons why we humans should ignore the *"teacup"* dog hype.

Reason 1: breeding ever smaller sized Yorkies (or any breed for that matter) is not going to be an improvement for the breed, because in order to breed smaller, it means breeding less healthy runts with runts, which generally produces weaker puppies with many health problems.

Reason 2: undersized Yorkies that weigh 4 pounds or less, generally live a much shorter life because they are especially prone to health problems such as chronic diarrhea and vomiting.

Reason 3: very small Yorkies will be more sensitive to anesthesia and much more difficult to operate on for the purposes of spaying or neutering because their organs are so tiny.

Reason 4: very small dogs can be much more easily injured, sometimes even breaking their legs simply from jumping off of a chair or out of the arms of someone holding them.

Reason 5: unscrupulous backyard or "Puppy Mill" operations are prime candidates for breeding small dogs because the entire

## Chapter 3: Teacupism

operation can take place in a smaller sized location.

Most registered breed clubs will work very long and hard to preserve the proper breed size standards for the health and wellbeing of the entire breed.

Responsible breeders would never purposefully breed their litters down in size to attain these ultra small sized Poms, because of the many associated health problems.

The extra small puppy or dog is a novelty, therefore, when we humans continue to buy them, the irresponsible breeders will continue to breed them, and runts of the litter will be bred with other runts in order to produce ever smaller dogs so that they can market them as "rare", at a very high price, to the unsuspecting or novelty-seeking public.

There are many questionable breeding practices associated with "teacup" sized dogs, and issues that begin long before they are even born.

This type of ultra-small breeding is a risky proposition for both the mother dog and the puppies themselves.

From the outset, the mother dog is so small, that it's unlikely that she will be able to produce any more than one or two puppies at the most, and with such tiny puppies there is a greatly increased chance of the puppies suffering from many complications.

There is much worse to come when the irresistible call of the almighty dollar gets in the way.

Tiny dogs in high demand can sell for many thousands of dollars, and this creates a very large incentive for unethical breeders to place the health of the mothers and puppies at serious risk.

When a breeder's top priority is making the largest profit possible, disreputable operations will produce the highly sought teacups any way they can, which often includes inbreeding of litters that

*Chapter 3: Teacupism*

are closely related as well as the cruel and inhumane practice of starving a puppy in the hope of stunting their growth.

As a result of there actually being no officially recognized teacup sized breed, fraud is another factor that becomes a problem, because it is very difficult to find a breeder who will guarantee that the puppy they are about to sell you will actually grow no larger than 4 pounds.

Sadly, it is all too easy amongst dishonest breeders to sell a puppy at a very young age, when it should still be with it's mother and then telling the prospective purchaser that the puppy is a teacup when in fact, it's a few weeks younger than what the bill of sale might indicate.

Unfortunately, the backyard or "puppy mill" breeding problem becomes even worse when responsible, reputable breeders refuse to sell teacup-sized puppies, because this leave the market wide open to those types of breeders whose only concern is a large dollar return.

## Severe Health Problems

Of course, every breed can be prone to certain diseases and disorders, however, the list of issues for teacup-sized dogs, including the Yorkie, can be lengthy as well as severe.

"Teacupism" creates health issues that are directly related to their unnaturally small size.

Next, there are problems that result from inbreeding and other questionable, inhumane practices of backyard and puppy mill breeders.

When all of the probable health issues begin to, teacups, as a group, tend not to live nearly as long as the breed standard size.

There are many articles written about teacup-sized breeds that discuss the very common occurrence of *"hypoglycemia"*, commonly referred to as low blood sugar, which can cause brain damage, seizures and premature death, if not noticed in time and carefully monitored.

Many of these ultra small dogs must be hand fed several times a day, and sometimes force fed if hypoglycemia is evident, and even if they are lucky enough not to suffer from this life-threatening condition, teacups are often plagued with digestive problems and poor appetite, which is a constant stress for themselves and their owners.

Other common health issues may include heart problems, water on the brain (hydrocephalus), liver shunts, or breathing problems. Anyone considering a teacup should factor in the potential for higher-than-normal veterinarian bills — not to mention all the worry, frustration and heartbreak that comes with owning a chronically ill pet.

If you are fortunate enough to have a fairly healthy Teacup Yorkie, you will have to closely monitor this tiny dog 24/7 simply because the ultra small size of this dog means that it will live in constant peril of accidentally being injured or maimed by any manner of life that is so much larger than itself.

Anyone who has ever lived with a very small dog may already understand some of the simple problems being short and more fragile can create.

For instance, a guardian for a ultra small sized dog must be always vigilant, as a Teacup Yorkie needs to be lifted on and off of most furniture and in and out of vehicles because they are too weak or fragile and too short and you don't want them to risk injuring themselves by trying to get up or down on their own.

Now imagine that your dog weighs less than four pounds and that everything in its world is towering over them and you might be able to imagine the world of a Teacup Yorkie.

When you stop for a moment to think about the life of a micro-

## Chapter 3: Teacupism

sized dog, it becomes obvious that these tiny dogs can be easily injured, especially when jumping down from a chair or couch or if they should squirm out of your arms and get dropped on the floor.

Teacup Yorkies will have much smaller and more fragile bones that can easily be broken. This makes a teacup-sized Yorkie a singularly scary choice for families with young children, who will all be fighting for the opportunity to carry around such an adorable little dog. This is a tragic accident waiting to happen.

As well, other dogs, particularly larger ones, may accidentally hurt such a small dog, even in play, and those larger dogs with high prey drive may look upon a teacup-sized Yorkies as some sort of rodent that they should kill with one swift bite. Indeed, the otherwise docile family cat also needs to be looked at in a different light, as they may not be trustworthy around such a tiny dog.

Most dogs have a tendency to get underfoot, and the same is true of the inquisitive, playful and feisty Yorkie, no matter what their size. What makes this problem worse is that you are much less likely to see a teacup-sized Yorkie, which means that you are much more likely to accidentally cause a serious injury by kicking them, stepping on them, dropping them or sitting on them.

**Important:**

You might think, "Hang on a minute, you are saying breeding Teacup Yorkies should not be encouraged, ever, but you are writing a book about it!".

I can see your reasoning and my answer is as follows: I know that a lot of people WILL buy teacup dogs, regardless. If you DO decide to buy a teacup Pom, please look after it as well as possible, as explained in this book. By writing a book about it, at least you are informed about the facts and the things you need to know before you buy.

## Chapter 3: Teacupism

**Things to be aware off when you decide to buy a Teacup Yorkie:**

- Your Yorkie is very likely to suffer, from an early age, because of poor health. However, you might be lucky and buy a dog that doesn't have any more problems than a normal sized Yorkie.

- Your Yorkie can grow much bigger than a "teacup sized dog".

- Your dog insurance might increase tremendously every year. The more vet treatments your dog will have in one year, the more your insurance will increase the next year. That's how the vast majority of pet insurance companies operate.

Even if you don't take your dog to the vet often, your dog insurance fee will still increase, the older your dog gets. Therefore, when you visit the vet often, which you are likely to do with a Teacup Yorkie, your fees will increase even more. Make sure you can afford the insurance fees!

> **If you haven't purchased a Teacup Yorkie yet, I advise you not to buy one, as otherwise, the breeders with nothing but dollar signs in their eyes will be encouraged to breed more.**

# Chapter 4: Breeding

The original breeding of the Yorkshire Terrier is attributed to the working Scottish people working in the cotton or woolen mills or in coalmines located in the counties of Yorkshire and Lancashire, England.

Unfortunately, as relatively uneducated mill operators and mine workers, who were unaccustomed to keeping public records, were the originators of the Yorkshire Terrier breed, breeding records were not kept during these early days, which easily explains why original breeding details for the Yorkie are somewhat scarce.

While accurate records were not kept of early breeding practices, it does seem to be agreed that the breed originated from a female terrier named *"Kitty"* and a male terrier named *"Old Crab.*

It is also understood that the long, silky coat of the Paisley terrier, which is a smaller version of the Skye terrier, was involved in the mix that created the early Yorkshire Terrier.

Further, some authorities believe that the Maltese was also part of the DNA pool that established this breed.

No matter the exact story, today's Yorkshire terriers were all originally bred from Scottish terriers from Scotland and originally shown under the name *"Scottish Terrier",* until the name was changed to *"Yorkshire Terrier"* as a result of the significant breed improvements having taken place in Yorkshire, England.

## 1. Father of the Breed

Before the breed became well established, any small dog in the size and shape of a terrier, with a short tail, and trimmed ears, that had a long blue coat with fawn or silver colored legs and head, was considered to be a Yorkshire Terrier. This trend continued until a very popular Paisley show terrier named "Huddersfield Ben" made his show scene appearance in the late 1860s.

Mary Ann Foster of Yorkshire, was the guardian of Ben, who was seen winning dog shows all over Great Britain, and it was Ben who was instrumental in defining the breed standard for the dog we now know as the Yorkshire Terrier.

## 2. Huddersfield Ben

According to Ben's pedigree, he was line bred, which means that he was the product of a mother-son breeding, just like his mother, "Lady".

Lady was the great-great-granddaughter of Mr. J. Swift's *"Old Crab"*, who was a long coated black and tan terrier born around 1850.

Some Yorkie fanciers believe that *"Old Crab"* and a Paisley terrier called *" Kitty"*, owned by J. Kershaw of West Yorkshire, hold the honor of being the first recorded predecessors of the modern Yorkshire Terrier breed.

Huddersfield Ben became an accomplished and famous show dog, winning 74 show prizes throughout his career, as well as ratting competitions, which made Ben exactly the type of dog that everybody was looking for.

Ben competed in Manchester in 1869 where he placed second,

*Chapter 4: Breeding*

and again at Manchester and the Crystal Palace in 1870 where he won first place, and in the following year, Ben took both first and second prizes.

George Earl, a prominent sporting dog painter, immortalized Ben in one of his portraits, and in 1891 a breed authority wrote that, *"Huddersfield Ben was the best stud dog of his breed during his lifetime, and one of the most remarkable dogs of any pet breed that ever lived."*

Most of the show specimens of the present day have one or more crosses of Ben's blood in their pedigree, and through his puppies, he has defined the Yorkshire Terrier breed as we know it today.

Even though Ben was considerably larger than the breed standard, weighing between 9 and 12 pounds (4 and 5 kilograms) he consistently sired litters of puppies that competed in the under 7 pound (under 3 kilogram) show category.

Some 464 years later, Huddersfield Ben, who was born around 1850, is still referred to as *"father of the breed."*

## 3. In North America

While the first Yorkshire Terrier was introduced to North America in 1872, thirteen more years passed before the American Kennel Club (AKC) registered the first Yorkshire Terrier.

The Yorkshire Terrier was a very popular small dog that was seen at many dog shows in England during the Victorian era, and as Americans were always quick to embrace Victorian customs, they also eagerly embraced the Yorkie.

The breed's popularity started to see a substantial decline around the 1940's when the percentage of registered small breed dogs dipped to an all-time low of just 18% of total Kennel Club registrations.

The Yorkie breed enjoyed a boost in popularity that has continued every since, when a story about a famous terrier from World War II, named Smoky, hit the airwaves.

## 4. Biewer Yorkie

In 1984, a piebald (meaning un-pigmented) Yorkshire Terrier containing large amounts of white in the coat was born as a result of breeding two Yorkies that both possessed a genetic recessive gene.

This rare white puppy was born in Germany on January 20, 1984 when breeding two Yorkshire Terriers together that were owned by Gertrud and Werner Biewer.

This white piebald puppy was called *"Snowflake"* and given the registered German name of *"Schneefloeckchen von Friedheck"*.

Today dogs with piebald coats are still considered a breed separate from other Yorkies, and are given the name *"Biewer"* or *"Biewer Yorkie"* after Werner Biewer.

## 5. Locating a Reputable Breeder

**NOTE**: this chapter is not about how to breed the Teacup Yorkie, rather it is all about how to care for each stage of the dog's life.

Although a good breeder cannot guarantee the lifelong health of any puppy, they should easily be able to provide a prospective Teacup Yorkie guardian with plenty of information about the health of the puppy's parents.

Prospective guardians should definitely ask the breeder what sort of health tests have been carried out on the parents of a puppy they may be considering purchasing.

For instance, a reputable breeder will have had their breeding dogs tested for hip, thyroid, eye or other problems inherent in the breed and prospective puppy purchasers should always inquire about possible congenital problems the parents or grandparents of the puppy might have, including any premature deaths.

## 6. Meet the Parents

Meeting the mother and father of your new Teacup Yorkie puppy can tell you a great deal about what the temperament and demeanor of your puppy will likely be when they grow into adulthood.

The Teacup Yorkie puppy's personality or temperament will be a combination of what they experience in the early days of their environment when they are in the breeder's care, and the genes inherited from both parents.

Visiting the breeder several times, observing the parents, interacting with the puppies and asking plenty of questions will help you to get a true feeling for the sincerity of the breeder.

The early environment provided by the breeder and the parents of the puppies can have a formative impact on how well your puppy will ultimately behave as an adult dog.

## 7. Questions to Ask a Breeder

Get to know your breeder by asking them why they decided to breed the Teacup Yorkie and how long they have been breeding.

Ask if the breeder will permit you to visit their facility and will they give you a tour?

Ask the breeder if they own both breeding parents, or if they do not, ask if they are familiar with, or have worked closely with both parents of the Teacup Yorkie puppy you may be considering. Ask how often the breeder allows the females and males to breed and reproduce.

## Chapter 4: Breeding

Ask if the breeder will allow you to see the other dogs in the kennel and notice whether the kennel is clean, well maintained and animal friendly.

Will the breeder permit you to see other adult dogs, or other puppies that the breeder owns, socialize together?

Pay attention to whether the breeder limits the amount of time that you are permitted to handle the Teacup Yorkie puppies. A reputable breeder will be concerned for the safety and health of all their puppies and will only permit serious buyers to handle the puppies.

Check to find out if the breeder is registered or recognized by your local, state or national breed organization.

**a) Medical Questions**

Every reputable breeder will certainly ensure that their Teacup Yorkie puppies have received vaccinations and de-worming specific to the age of the puppies.

Always ask the breeder what shots the puppy has received and when it was last de-wormed and ask for the name of the breeder's veterinarian.

If you discover that the breeder has not carried out any of these procedures or they are unable to tell you when the last shots or de-worming was carried out, look elsewhere.

Also ask to see the breeder's veterinarian report on the health of the puppy you may be interested in purchasing, and if they cannot produce this report, look elsewhere.

## b) Temperament Questions

You will want to choose a puppy with a friendly, easy going and congenial temperament and your breeder should be able to help you with your selection.

A good breeder will have noticed personality and temperament traits very early on in their Teacup Yorkie puppies and should be able to provide a prospective purchaser with valuable insight concerning each puppy's unique personality.

Also ask the breeder about the temperament and personalities of the puppy's parents and ask what they have done to socialize the puppies.

Ask how old the puppies must be before they can be taken to their new homes. If the breeder is willing to let their puppies go any earlier than 10 weeks of age, they are more interested in making a profit than in the health of their puppies. Always be certain to ask if a Teacup Yorkie puppy you are interested in has displayed any signs of aggression or fear, because if this is happening at such an early age, you may experience behavioral troubles when the puppy becomes older.

## c) Guarantee Questions

A reputable Teacup Yorkie breeder will be interested in the lifelong health and wellbeing of all of their puppies and good breeders will want you to call them should a problem arise at any time during the life of your Teacup Yorkie puppy.

As well, a good breeder will want you to return a puppy or dog to them, if for some reason you are unable to continue to care for it, rather than seeing the dog go to a shelter or rescue facility. If the Teacup Yorkie breeder you are considering does not offer this type of return policy, find one who does, because no ethical breeder would ever permit a puppy from one of his or her litters to end up in a shelter.

## Chapter 4: Breeding

### d) Return Contract

Reputable breeders offer return contracts. They do this to protect their reputation and to also make sure that a puppy they have sold that might display a genetic defect will not have the opportunity to breed and continue to spread the defect, which could weaken the entire breed.

Many breeders also offer return contracts because purchasing a hybrid Teacup Yorkie puppy from a breeder can be an expensive proposition, and if you find out that the puppy has a worrisome genetic defect, this could cost you a great deal with respect to unexpected veterinarian care. In such cases, most good breeders offer a return policy, and will be happy to give you another puppy.

### e) Testimonials

Ask the Teacup Yorkie breeder you are considering to provide you with testimonials from some of their previous clients, and then actually contact those people to ask them about their experience with the breeder, and the health and temperament of their Teacup Yorkie dog. A good breeder has nothing to hide and will be more than happy to provide you with testimonials because their best recommendation is a happy customer.

### f) Breeder Reputation

The Internet can be a valuable resource when researching the reputation of a Teacup Yorkie breeder. For instance, you will be able to post on most forums discussing breeders to quickly find out what you need to know from those who have firsthand experience.

Also, be prepared to answer questions the breeder may have for you, because a reputable breeder will want to ask a prospective

## Chapter 4: Breeding

purchaser their own questions, so that they can satisfy themselves that you are going to be a good caretaker for their puppy.

First, do your homework about the Teacup Yorkie breed and then carry out as much research as possible about the specific breeder you are considering before making your initial visit to their facility. The more information you have gathered about the Teacup Yorkie breed, and the breeder you are considering and the more information the breeder knows about you, the more successful the match will be.

# Chapter 5: Vital Statistics

## 1. Country of Origin

Even though England is often noted as the country of origin, it was Scottish mill and mine workers who first bred these dogs and who brought the ancestors of the original Yorkie with them when they travelled from Scotland to northern England.

Therefore, while the breed was further developed in Yorkshire, many would argue that Scotland (where the breed was called the "Scotch" terrier), should more rightfully noted as the country of origin.

## 2. Litter Size

While litter size can vary in number between one and five puppies, on average there will be four or less puppies born to a teacup-sized mother.

## 3. Height and Weight

The size and weight of a Yorkie will depend on the size of the breeding parents. When measured at the withers (top of the shoulder), a teacup sized Yorkie will be between 4 and 6 inches (10.16 and 15.24 centimeters) and ideally weigh 4 pounds or less (1.81 kilograms or less).

Many Yorkies sold as "teacups" will grow to be considerably larger than expected, which, as far as their health is concerned, is a good thing.

It is good advice to always steer clear of breeders who are offering a "teacup" sized Yorkie for sale, because these are extremely undersized dogs that will be prone to many disorders that could lead to a very short life.

*Chapter 4: Vital Statistics*

## 4. Temperature & Heart Rate

Temperature: 100.5 to 102.5 degrees Fahrenheit (38.05 to 39.16 Celsius).

Respiratory Rate: 10 to 20 per minute

Pulse: Puppies, 120 to 160 per minute. Adults, 60 to 140 per minute.

Gums: should be pink

## 5. Lifespan

On average, the lifespan of a healthy dog will be between 12 and 15 years or even longer. Many teacup-sized Yorkies may live a shorter lifespan.

The record for the oldest recorded living Yorkshire Terrier goes to a Yorkie named *"Billy"*, who is 22-years-old. Billy, who is the current holder of the Guinness World Record, is believed to be 154 years old in human years.

Also, a Yorkie named *"Bonny"* is reported to be as old as 28 years, which is 196 in human years.

## 6. Intelligence

Stanley Coren, a professor of psychology at the University of British Columbia, in Vancouver, B.C., Canada, published **The Intelligence of Dogs** in 1994. Since then this book has become the standard for rating the particular intelligence of different canine breeds.

Coren's book describes three categories of dog intelligence:

  (1) *instinctive intelligence*;

## Chapter 4: Vital Statistics

 (2) *adaptive intelligence*, and

 (3) *working and obedience intelligence...*

where he indicates that"

*"Instinctive intelligence refers to a dog's ability to carry out tasks it was bred to perform, such as guarding, herding, hunting, pointing, retrieving, or supplying companionship."*

Coren further notes that:

*"Adaptive intelligence refers to how well a dog is able to solve problems on its own.*

*"Working and obedience intelligence refers to how quickly a dog is able to learn from humans."*

In other words, if one is to agree with the findings of Stanley Coren, the Yorkshire Terrier ranks in the #27 position out of a total 79 breeds tested, in the above average working dog category. According to Coren, this means that the Yorkie can understand new commands after 15 to 25 repetitions and will obey first commands approximately *"70% of the time, or better"*.

Please keep in mind that there are always exceptions to every study and a particular breed's degree of intelligence can often be related to their early upbringing and how they are socialized and trained. The Yorkie will be an intelligent, active and amusing little companion that will be easy to train and will enjoy learning new things and as much activity as their guardian can provide.

## 7. Living Conditions

The Yorkie does not need a large living space and will do well in smaller living conditions, such as an apartment or condominium, so long as you get them outside regularly.

## Chapter 4: Vital Statistics

While within every litter of puppies there will also be great differences in activity levels, generally speaking, the Yorkshire Terrier, being a tenacious little terrier, originally bred to be a working dog that hunts and kills vermin, they will need lots of daily exercise to stay fit, happy and healthy.

Don't be fooled by their small size, because although they can get exercise running about inside, they need to know that you are the boss, which means that these are active dogs that will require a minimum of two to three daily 30 minute, disciplined walks on leash with you as their leader.

The smaller size of the Yorkshire Terrier is often appealing to those who live in apartments or condominiums because they can be trained to use a litter box, potty patch or pee pad. Even if you do train a Yorkie to bathroom inside, they will always prefer to go outside for a walk with you.

This toy-sized terrier can be sensitive to the cold and many will prefer warmer climates, or a sunny window to warm themselves on colder days.

If you live in a climate that experiences icy winters, you will want to make sure that you have the appropriate warm outerwear for this little terrier to wear when exercising outside in cold or rainy weather.

If you live where the winters are extremely harsh, you may want to consider training your Yorkie to use a litter box, potty patch or pee pad because many of these little dogs may flatly refuse to go outside if the weather is not agreeable to them.

Every dog has a primal instinct to roam and walk their territory, no matter what their size, and without these daily walks this intelligent little dog may begin to display behavior problems.

A good rule of thumb for determining whether your tiny Yorkie is

## Chapter 4: Vital Statistics

receiving enough walk time with you is to take notice whether your dog is constantly bouncing around your apartment or house like a ricocheting pinball. If they are, they need more disciplined exercise or longer walks on leash.

Whether you are outside in the yard or out and about in the neighborhood, it is a good idea to keep your Teacup Yorkie on a leash because they are very good at escaping from fenced yards, love to chase things and will not hesitate to pick a fight with a bigger dog, and in the case of a Teacup York, most every other dog will be bigger.

As well, this tiny dog can easily be prey for large birds that may swoop in and carry them off.

This is not a dog that you will want to leave home alone for many hours every day as they will be very attached to their guardians and it will be torture for them that could result in the Yorkie making its own entertainment by becoming destructive and/or noisy.

## Chapter 6: Temperament

A Yorkie is almost certainly going to be an energetic, intelligent dog that loves to run and play and learn new tricks and commands and demanding of spending all its time with you.

Every dog needs the discipline of being walked on leash outside of the home each day, as well as the opportunity for off leash time to run and play fetch or enjoy socializing with other dogs.

Yorkies are very alert and make excellent watchdogs, although if not trained at an early age can become incessant barkers.

Although small in stature, the ideal Yorkshire Terrier character or *"personality"* will be larger than life, which is one of the reasons this tiny toy breed remains one of the most popular in the canine world.

The Yorkie is a happy and amusing companion carrying itself with a bouncy, upright, energetic gait that exudes fun loving confidence.

This charming little dog is a forever curious, always active, attention seeking and amusing small companion that will certainly keep you laughing.

While the personality of every Yorkie will be different and they will develop traits and quirks that are unique to each dog, depending on the temperament of the parents, the home where they are raised and how they are socialized, most Yorkshire Terriers will tend to be energetic and spirited, which is usually a common trait of terrier breeds.

These little dogs have truly made a most remarkable transition from working rat killers to canine socialites who revel in all the attention they can get, which makes them great companions for those who can give them the daily attention they crave more than

## Chapter 6: Temperament

anything else.

Many guardians will agree that their little companions will faithfully follow them from room to room as if attached by an invisible umbilical cord, because they just don't like to be left alone.

Although the Yorkie can be a happy family dog, since they are so attention loving, they also make superior companions for older, retired folks who are able to focus all of their energy on this sweet, little dog.

Some guardians will also agree that the Teacup Yorkie is not shy about being heard and can be quite vocal, which makes them good little watch dogs who quickly sound the alarm whenever they hear unfamiliar noises or a stranger approaching the home.

This tiny Yorkie is well known for having big dog attitude in a very small dog body. This feisty fur ball will seemingly disregard their own small stature and bravely approach any other dog, no matter their size, without thinking twice about it.

This affectionate and highly energetic bundle of energy is always eager for adventure, which makes them entertaining and fun loving companions who are ever ready for their next outing.

Properly socializing a Yorkshire Terrier early on, during the first three months of its life, will greatly influence the dog's temperament, personality and behavior as it matures into adulthood.

Continuing to shape the personality of the dog through adolescence and on into adulthood with proper socializing will ensure a well-mannered dog.

The Yorkie will be a good family dog for retired folks or families with older children, as they will be affectionate and totally devoted to the family.

Plenty of exercise will be a highly necessary part of their daily life, so that they can eliminate pent up energy, exercise their minds and their bodies and remain a healthy weight.

## 1. Behavior With Children and Pets

Generally speaking, while the Teacup Yorkie will be a good choice for active families with older children, as this is a smaller than average sized toy breed, they may not be a good choice for families with young children who could accidentally injure them.

This is a dog that can be very excitable, who really needs a structured living situation and a regular exercise routine in order to prevent anxiety related behavioral problems.

Yorkshire Terrier puppies need to become accustomed to human touch, different voices, other animals and environments early on in life so that they become comfortable in all circumstances.

Those who decide to share their home with one of these intelligent small bundles of joy will need to make sure that they also provide the dog with leadership so that it does not develop unwanted habits, such as aggressive behavior, as it matures into an adult dog.

## 2. Toy Dogs Can Be Prey

Be aware if you are living in or are visiting an area where wildlife is abundant, or even in populated cities where hawks are known to be nesting.

When exercising your Yorkie, always keep in mind that toy sized dogs can be easy prey for large predator birds, such as eagles, hawks and owls as well as larger wild animals, including big cats (cougars, mountain lions, bobcats), coyotes, and wolves.

Also, if you are visiting the desert, you will need to be aware of poisonous snakes, spiders and scorpions, especially since the

*Chapter 6: Temperament*

Yorkshire Terrier has a natural tendency to want to chase things that disappear down holes.

As well, if you are visiting a part of the world that is populated by crocodiles or vacationing in Florida or southeastern parts of the United States, or the Yangtze River in China, that has a high population of alligators, you will need to keep your dog away from this very real danger.

## 3. Is This Dog an Escape Artist?

When considering the Yorkie, remember that this is a terrier breed, which may excel at digging their way to freedom if given enough time and left alone in a yard.

The terrier receives its name from the Latin word *"terra"*, which means earth, and is a reference to a terrier's love of digging in the ground in the pursuit of small prey, such as rats, moles, badgers, etc.

This dog should never be left alone or unsupervised outside, even in a securely fenced yard because as well as being easy dinner for a large bird of prey, and their possibly being talented diggers, their small size makes it easy for them to slip through cracks in fences or crawl underneath.

Of course, all dogs will have a much higher urge to roam before they are spayed or neutered, therefore, early spaying or neutering of a Yorkie puppy will go a long way toward helping to curb any wanderlust tendencies that may be a result of raging hormones.

# Chapter 7: Before You Buy

## Pros and Cons

No matter what breed you may be considering as a possible candidate for sharing your home and life, this decision should never be entered into lightly.

As with any breed, those who may be considering a Teacup Yorkie need to carry out research and make sure they have all the facts straight before taking the plunge because there are always many important factors to keep in mind.

Yorkies are loving, intelligent, active small athletes who will enjoy any sort of advanced training or obedience competition, such as Agility, Rally or Trick Training.

The terrier tenacity of this toy breed can make them a little more dominant, independent or strong willed, which means that they may do best with a firmer hand.

When treated kindly and trained with positive reinforcement, the Yorkie will have a zest for learning new things very quickly and will love the attention any sort of training program provides.

If you are often away from home, this breed is not a good choice for you because the Yorkie is very attached to their guardians and can easily become upset when left alone for long periods, which could display itself by barking and destructive behavior.

If expected to stay at home alone for long periods of time, this is not the dog for you, because the Yorkie wants to always be with their guardian.

## Chapter 7: Before You Buy

This is a dog that will do well with active families with older children, or active seniors who prefer an alert, energetic and loving small dog.

## 1. Pros of Yorkie Ownership

The Yorkie has many good qualities to consider, including:

- Playful and energetic;
- Entertaining and loving;
- Non or low shedding coat;
- They do well in smaller living spaces;
- Easy to transport in a Sherpa bag;
- They love to participate in canine sports;
- They may live a long life;
- Intelligent and easy to train;
- Excellent watch dogs;

## 2. Cons of Yorkie Ownership

No matter what breed you choose, there will always be some downsides to carefully consider, including:

- When a hybrid becomes popular, like the Yorkie, this is all it takes for unscrupulous puppy mill breeders, who care nothing about the health or temperament of the puppies they are breeding, to get on the bandwagon;

## Chapter 7: Before You Buy

- This is an active dog requiring daily exercising to keep them both physically and mentally healthy;

- They may like to dig;

- They may chase rodents or other small vermin;

- They require regular grooming;

- They require lifting off and onto furniture, in and out of vehicles and most objects taller than themselves;

- Guardians must be ever vigilant to not let this tiny dog jump from any height as their bones can easily be broken;

- They may bark and be destructive when left alone;

- Without the proper training, they can become dominant, aggressive, possessive of their guardians and/or difficult to handle;

- When left alone they may become noisy barkers;

- They need to be carefully watched or kept on leash when outside in case of predator birds or animals;

- Play with larger dogs must be closely monitored to prevent accidental injury;

- This tiny dog may not be a good choice for low energy, older guardians as they can be high energy, and although they do not require a big space, they do require plenty of daily exercise;

# Chapter 8: Choosing the Right Dog

## 1. Where to Purchase a US Puppy

When wondering where to start your search for purchasing a Teacup Yorkie puppy in the United States, first check clubs and breeders in your local area.

**North Carolina Yorkies** (North Carolina): *"Our dogs live with us in our home. They are able to socialize with each other, our cats and other visitors."*

**Rhapsody Yorkshire Terriers** (Michigan) is a Yorkie breeders website where *"Yorkshire Terriers have been part of my life for many years now, and I can't imagine being without them. Not only are they part of my life, but true companions and friends."*

## 2. Where to Purchase a UK Puppy

**Champ Dogs**, is a UK Yorkshire Terrier breeders website where many UK Yorkie breeders can register.

**The Kennel Club** is a comprehensive network of information and resources listing UK Yorkshire Terrier breeders by county.

## 3. Average Prices for Puppies

There is a wide range of *"average"* pricing for any designer or hybrid Teacup Yorkie, with some adoptions or rescues beginning around $300. (£179.).

If there is such a thing as an "average" breeder pricing for Yorkie puppies, the range will begin somewhere around $800. and go as high as $3,000. (£470. and £1,753.) or more, depending on the size of the puppy and the expertise of the particular breeder you are purchasing from. Generally speaking, the smaller the puppy, the higher the price tag.

**Important Note:** the authors of this book have not purchased dogs from all the breeders mentioned in this book. Make sure that you thoroughly research a breeder before buying a dog from them. There are a many dog breeders trading purely for profit and these often will not be overly concerned about the well being of the dogs they breed.

## 4. Avoiding Puppy Mills or Farms

As soon as a particular breed of dog becomes popular, they also become particularly susceptible to being bred by disreputable, high profit *"puppy mills"* or *"commercial breeding farms"*.

Puppy Mill breeding is especially prevalent with cute, smaller breeds, such as the Teacup Yorkie when bred with a toy or miniature parents.

This inhumane and cruel world of canine pregnancy for profit occurs all over the world, and if you are not very careful about where and how you purchase your Teacup Yorkie puppy, you may unknowingly end up promoting this disreputable practice.

Not only do Puppy Mills seriously contribute to overpopulation, they produce diseases, and genetically flawed puppies that may suffer greatly with behavioral and/or health related problems that will cost their guardians greatly in terms grief and stress and unexpected financial burden associated with veterinarian and behavioral costs, while the puppy's life may be cut prematurely short.

These dogs suffer in ways most of us could never imagine. For instance, most of these poor breeding dogs have never walked on solid ground or felt grass as they are housed in cramped wire cages their entire short lives.

*Chapter 8: Choosing the Right Dog*

Females are bred continuously until they can no longer produce puppies at which time they are sold to laboratories for experiments, killed or dumped on the side of a road.

Although the puppy mill problem is certainly not exclusive to the United States, as it happens all over the world, the problem is so rampant in the US that several states are actually labeled as "Puppy Mill States". These include Missouri, Nebraska, Kansas, Iowa, Arkansas, Oklahoma and Pennsylvania.

It can be difficult to shut down these mill or mass-producing farming operations because, just like the drug trade, it is business on a large and lucrative scale.

Although Puppy Mill puppies are sold in a variety of different venues, pet stores are the main source for selling these unfortunate puppies, who are taken away from their mothers far too young (at 4 to 5 weeks of age) and sold to brokers, who pack them into crates to ship them off to pet stores. Many innocent puppies die during transportation.

Think seriously before buying a puppy from a pet store because almost all puppies found in pet stores (whether or not the employees working there are aware of it) are the result of inhumane puppy mill breeding. If you purchase one of these puppies, you are helping to enable and perpetuate this horribly cruel breeding practice.

Every time someone buys a puppy from a pet store, the store will order more from the Puppy Mill. As far as the pet store is concerned, the puppies are simply inventory, like bags of dog food, and when one item drops off of the inventory list, another is purchased to replace it.

Puppy Mill puppies are also sold at flea markets, on the side of the road, at the beach, through newspaper ads and through fancy websites and Internet classifieds.

*Chapter 8: Choosing the Right Dog*

The only way to put these shameful, commercial businesses out of business is by spreading the word and never buying a puppy from a pet store, or any other advertising medium, unless you have first thoroughly checked them out by visiting the facility in person.

Always be wary if you answer an advertisement for a low priced puppy for sale and the person selling offers to deliver the puppy to you, because this could easily be the first sign that you are about to be involved in an illegal Puppy Mill operation.

Educate yourself and spread the word to others about Puppy Mills, because this is the first step toward ensuring that yourself and everyone you know are never unknowingly involved in the suffering that is forced upon the breeding dogs and puppies trapped in a puppy mill or mass farming operation.

## 5. How to Choose the Right Puppy

Choosing the <u>right</u> puppy for your family and your lifestyle is more important than you might imagine.

Many people do not give serious enough thought to sharing their home with a new puppy before they actually bring one home.

For instance, many of us choose a puppy solely based on what it looks like, because the breed may currently be popular, or because their family had the same kind of dog when they were growing up.

### a) Important Questions

In order to be fair to ourselves, our family and the puppy we choose to share our lives with, we humans need to take a serious look at our life, both as it is today and what we envision it being in the next ten to fifteen years, and then ask ourselves a few important, personal questions, and honestly answer them, before making the commitment to a puppy, including:

## Chapter 8: Choosing the Right Dog

Do I have the time and patience necessary to devote to a puppy, which will grow into a dog who needs a great deal of attention, training and endless amounts of my devotion?

Do I lead a physically active, medium or low intensity life? For instance, am I out jogging the streets daily or climbing mountains or would I rather spend my leisure time on the couch?

Do I like to travel a lot? Perhaps a dog small enough to travel in the plane cabin with me is a consideration.

Am I a neat freak? A low or non-shedding breed, such as the Teacup Yorkie, would make more sense.

Do I have a young, growing family that takes up all my spare time? A dog needs a lot of time and attention.

Am I physically fit and healthy enough to be out there walking a dog two to three times a day, every day, rain or shine (and much more when it's just a puppy)?

Can I afford the food costs and the veterinarian expenses that are part of being a conscientious dog guardian?

Is the decision to bring a puppy into my life a family decision, or just for the children, who will quickly lose interest?

Have I researched the breed I'm interested in, and is it compatible with my lifestyle?

What is the number one reason why I want a dog in my life?

Once you ask yourself these important questions and honestly answer them, you will have a much better understanding of the type of puppy that would be best suited for you and your family, and whether or not, it should be a Teacup Yorkie.

## Chapter 8: Choosing the Right Dog

If you are too busy for a dog, or choose the wrong dog, you will inevitably end up with an unhappy dog, which will lead to behavioral issues, which then will lead to an unhappy family and extra expense to hire a professional to help you reverse unwanted behavioral problems. Please take the time to choose wisely.

If you have absolutely decided that the Teacup Yorkie is the right dog for you, the following tips will help you to choose the right puppy from the litter.

**b) Careful Puppy Selection**

Although your breeder can often help you with selecting the right puppy for you and your family, you will likely be feeling especially drawn to one puppy over another.
Although there are other considerations, how you feel toward a particular puppy in a litter is also an important part of deciding which pup to bring home.

Beyond your feelings, considering other factors will help improve the odds of you having a positive guardianship experience with your new Teacup Yorkie puppy.

For instance, being a little objective when evaluating each puppy in the litter will help you to make the right choice.

While some people become very emotional when choosing a puppy and will be attracted to those who display extremes in behavior because they want to *"save"* them, it is not a particularly good idea to choose a puppy that may be very shy or frightened in the hope that they may grow into a happy, well-behaved dog.

Some people will delve even further into their emotional desires or needs to *"save"* or *"rescue"* and will choose a particular puppy because it has obvious health or behavioral issues, and because they want to provide it with a chance that they believe the puppy might not otherwise have.

## Chapter 8: Choosing the Right Dog

While it is certainly wonderful that we humans have the capacity to raise and care for puppies that may be afflicted with health or behavior problems, it's important that these types of decisions are not undertaken lightly as such challenges can lead you down a path that could be an emotional roller coaster of highs and lows that can cause problems for both canine and human alike.

While many minor behavioral problems can be modified with early training, it's important to be aware that the time and effort needed to do so will be difficult to predict and you should be aware that *"rescuing"* a dog that could grow up to have behavioral problems may require the services of a professional dog whisperer or psychologist.

### c) Pick of the Litter

Generally speaking, when choosing a puppy out of a litter, look for one that is friendly and outgoing, rather than one who is overly aggressive or fearful.

Taking note of a puppy's social skills, when they are still with their litter mates, will help you to choose the right puppy to take home because puppies who demonstrate good social skills with their litter mates are much more likely to develop into easy going, happy adults who play well with other dogs.

In a social setting where all the puppies can be observed together, make the following observations:

- When the puppies are playing, notice which puppies are comfortable both on top and on the bottom when play fighting and wresting with their littermates, and which puppies seem to only like being on top. Puppies who don't mind being on the bottom or who appear to be fine with either position, will usually play well with other dogs when they become adults.

- If the puppies have toys to play with, observe which puppies try to keep the toys away from the other puppies and which puppies share. Those who want to hoard the toys and keep all other puppies away may be more aggressive with other dogs over food or treats, or in play where toys are involved as they become older.

- Notice which puppies seem to like the company of the other pups and which ones seem to be loners. Puppies who like the company of their littermates are more likely to be interested in the company of other dogs as they mature than anti-social puppies.

- Observe the reaction of puppies that get yelped at when they bite or roughhouse with another puppy too hard. Puppies who ease up when another puppy yelps or cries are more likely to respond appropriately when they play too roughly as adults.

Also, check to see if the puppy you are interested in is sociable with people, because if they will not come to you, or display fear to strangers, this may be a problem when they become adults.

Further, always check if the puppy you are interested in is relaxed about being handled, because if they are not, they may become difficult with adults and children during daily interactions, during grooming or visits to the veterinarian's office.

## 6. How to Check If a Puppy is Healthy

Of course you will want to check if a puppy you are considering taking home is not just emotionally healthy, but also physically healthy.

First, ask to see veterinarian reports from the breeder to satisfy yourself that the puppy is as healthy as possible, and then once you make your decision to share your life with a particular puppy,

## Chapter 8: Choosing the Right Dog

make an appointment with your own veterinarian for a complete examination.

Before you get to this stage, however, there are a few general signs of good health to be aware of when choosing a healthy puppy from a litter, including the following:

- **Breathing** -- a healthy puppy will breathe quietly, without coughing or sneezing, and there will be no crusting or discharge around their nostrils;

- **Body** -- they will look round and well fed, with an obvious layer of fat over their rib cage;

- **Coat** – a healthy puppy will have a soft coat with no dandruff, dullness, greasiness or bald spots;

- **Energy** -- a well rested puppy will be alert and energetic;

- **Hearing** -- a healthy puppy with good hearing should react if you clap your hands behind their head;

- **Genitals** -- a healthy puppy will not have any sort of discharge visible in or around their genital or anal regions;

- **Mobility** – a healthy puppy will walk and run normally without wobbling, limping or seeming to be weak, stiff or sore; and

- **Vision**: -- a healthy puppy will have bright, clear eyes without crust or discharge and they should notice if a ball is rolled past them within their field of vision.

## 7. One Teacup Yorkie, or Two?

While getting two Teacup Yorkie puppies at once will be twice the fun, it will also be twice the work which means that you will

## Chapter 8: Choosing the Right Dog

need to be doubly alert and patient, and perhaps also lose even more sleep than you bargained for during the potty training phase.

Every puppy needs your constant attention and guidance, therefore, before taking the plunge, ask yourself if you have the time and energy to provide constant attention and guidance for two little puppies that could be running in opposite directions?

Many humans decide to get two puppies because they want their puppy to have someone to play with. Be careful that one of the reasons for this decision is not based on the fact that the human making this decision might not be the ideal candidate for having one puppy, let alone two.

For instance, if the reason you are considering two puppies is so that the one puppy will not be alone all day while you are at work, stop right there, because leaving one, two or a dozen puppies alone all day while you are at work is a terrible decision.

If this is your situation, you should NOT be considering any puppy at this stage of your life, and especially not one as loving and connected to their guardians as a Teacup Yorkie who will suffer severely by being left alone

Another consideration when thinking about whether or not to get two puppies is that often when they grow up, there may be continual sibling rivalry as each puppy vies for your attention.

It is entirely possible that when the puppies mature, they will no longer get along with each as well as they once did when they were young puppies.

Further, when you have two puppies growing up together, one will always be the more dominant personality that will take over the other, and this could mean that neither puppy will fully develop their individual personalities.

*Chapter 8: Choosing the Right Dog*

As well, when you have two puppies or dogs in your life, they generally tend to be less affectionate or interested in their human guardians as they have each other in their own pack of dogs to rely upon. This can mean that they will focus so much on each other that they will bond much less with you, which can make it more difficult to train or convince either that you are the actual leader of the pack.

Each puppy will require your individual attention when it comes time for training, and having two puppies in the picture can make it very difficult for them to concentrate or focus on the job at hand.

For instance, when you are teaching puppy #1 to "Sit" while puppy #2 is trying to bite the tail of puppy #1, your job is going to be much more challenging.

Bottom line, most professional trainers or psychologists will advise that if you want two puppies, not to get them at the exact same time, from the same litter, so that you have the opportunity to house train and teach basic commands to one puppy before you bring another one into the home.

## 8. Best Age to Purchase a Puppy

Generally speaking, no puppy, including a Teacup Yorkie puppy, should be removed from their mother any earlier than 8 weeks of age and leaving them until they are **10 to 16 weeks of age is preferred** because this will give them the extra time to learn important life skills from the mother dog, including eating solid food and grooming.

As well, leaving a puppy amongst their littermates for a longer period of time will help to ensure that they learn socialization skills.

Removing a puppy from the mother and other siblings too early could mean that they will miss out on valuable skills, and may not socialize well with others.

For the first month of a puppy's life they will be on a mother's milk only diet. Once the puppy's teeth begin to appear, they will start to be weaned from mother's milk and by the age of 8 weeks should be completely weaned and eating just puppy food.

Removing a puppy from their mother any earlier than eight weeks could mean they are not fully weaned and they would be much more difficult to feed.

## 9. Should I Get a Male or Female?

Everyone you ask will have a personal opinion about whether you should get a male or a female of any breed.

While you will find just as many humans preferring a male Teacup Yorkie over a female Teacup Yorkie, if you are a first time dog guardian, there may be a few considerations that can help you to make a more informed decision.

For instance, male dogs tend to want to mark or pee on anything upright (trees, telephone poles, tall grass, a stranger's leg) wherever they are out walking much more than females, however, a dominant female will also pee on three legs in an attempt to mark territory.

A male Teacup Yorkie, even a housebroken one, may try to lift their leg on furniture when visiting a home where there are other dogs present.

When spaying and neutering your Teacup Yorkie, the operation is much more invasive when spaying a female than the neutering process required for males.

## Chapter 8: Choosing the Right Dog

Some humans pick their dogs based on sex alone because they cannot stop themselves from attributing human characteristics to their chosen dogs, and therefore believe that, for instance, a female dog will have a *"sweeter"* temperament, or a male dog may be more *"independent"*.

Of course, this is complete nonsense, because a dog is a dog, and it can be harmful to your relationship to project human emotions onto them or imagine that they will act like humans just because we are human.

Therefore, the best way to choose your Teacup Yorkie puppy will be to take your time observing the litter when you visit the breeder.

## 10. The Teacup Yorkie Shopping List

Before bringing home your new Teacup Yorkie for the first time, there will be a list of items you need to make sure you have on hand, including:

- Food – usually the puppy will remain on whatever food they have been fed at the breeder's for at least the first couple of weeks, until they are well settled in their new home, so make sure you ask the breeder what brand to buy;

- Food and Water Bowls – make sure they are small enough for a young Teacup Yorkie puppy to get into so that they can easily eat and drink.

- Kennel – when you buy your puppy's hard-sided kennel, make sure that you buy the size that will be appropriate for them when they are full grown. It must be large enough so that (when full grown) they can easily stand up and turn around inside it;

*Chapter 8: Choosing the Right Dog*

- Soft Sided Sherpa – for easy transportation of smaller dogs. Make sure you buy the size they will need when they are full grown;

- Martingale Collar, 2 Leashes and Harness – buy the harness and collar small enough to fit your puppy and buy new collars as they grow larger.

- Leashes – you will be able to keep the same leashes as all you will ever need is a four foot (1.22 meters) leash made out of nylon webbing with a light weight clip at the end (do not buy a leash that has a heavy clip on the end as it will be difficult for your puppy to carry around;

- Soft Beds (one or two) – for them to sleep in when they are not in their kennel. Buy the beds large enough for a full grown Teacup Yorkie;

- Canine Shampoo and Conditioner;

- Finger Tooth Brush –- this is a soft rubber cap that fits over the human's finger to get the puppy used to having their teeth regularly brushed;

- Soft Bristle Brush or Comb for longer coats – for daily grooming;

- Puppy Nail Scissors – for trimming their toenails, and a medium or large-sized pair of plier style nail clippers for when they are full grown;

- One or two Soft Toys -- or wait until they come home and let them pick their own toys from the store;

- Puppy sized Treats;

*Chapter 8: Choosing the Right Dog*

- Poop Bags;

- Pee Pads;

- Bath Towels;

- Non-slip Mat for the sink or tub.

Be sure to take your Teacup Yorkie shopping list with you when you go to your local pet store or boutique, otherwise you may forget critical items.

**NOTE**: if you do not already have a hairdryer, you will need to get one of these, too, so you can dry your puppy after bath time.

## 11. Puppy Proofing Your Home

Most puppies will be a curious bundle of energy, eager to explore everything, which means that they will get into everything within their reach.

As a responsible puppy guardian, you will want to provide a safe environment for them, which means eliminating all sources of danger, similar to what you would do for a curious toddler.

Be aware that your Teacup Yorkie puppy will want to touch, sniff, taste, chew, investigate and closely inspect every electrical cord, every closet, every nook and cranny of your home and everything you may have left lying about on the floor.

Power cords can be found in just about every room in the home and to a teething puppy, these may look like irresistible, fun, chew toys. Make sure that you tuck all power cords securely out of your puppy's reach or enclose them inside a chew-proof PVC tube.

**Kitchen** – first of all, there are many human foods that can be harmful to dogs, therefore, your kitchen should always be strictly off limits to your puppy any time you are preparing food.

Calmly send them out of the kitchen any time you are in the kitchen, and they will quickly get the idea that this area is off limits to them.

**Bathroom** – bathroom cupboards and drawers or the side of a bathtub where you may leave your shaving supplies can hold many dangers for a young and curious Teacup Yorkie puppy.

Kleenex, cotton swabs, Q-tips, toilet paper, razors, pills, soap or other materials left within your puppy's reach are an easy target that could result in an emergency visit to your veterinarian's office.

Family members need to put shampoos, soap, facial products, makeup and accessories out of reach or safely inside a cabinet or drawer.

**Bedroom** – if you don't keep your shoes, slippers and clothing safely behind doors, you may find that your puppy has claimed them for their new chew toys.

Be vigilant about keeping everything in its safe place, including jewelry, hair ties, bills, coins, and other items small enough for them to swallow in containers or drawers, and secure any exposed cords or wires.

If you have children, make sure they understand that, especially while your puppy is going through their teething stage, they must keep their rooms picked up and leave nothing that could cause a choking problem to the puppy lying about on the floor or within their reach.

**Living Room** – we humans spend many hours in our cozy gathering places to watch movies or play games, and often the living areas of our homes will have many items that are very

## Chapter 8: Choosing the Right Dog

enticing for a curious and teething puppy, such as books, magazines, pillows, iPods, cell phones, TV remotes and more.

You will want to keep your home free of excess clutter and remain vigilant about straightening up and putting things out of sight that could be tempting to your puppy.

**Office** – we humans often spend a great deal of time in our home offices, which means that our puppy will want to be there, too, and they will be curious about all the items an office has to offer, such as cell phones, papers, books, magazines, and electrical cords.

Although your puppy might think that rubber bands or paper clips are fun to play with, allowing these items to be within your puppy's reach could end up being a fatal mistake if your puppy swallows them.

**Plants**: – can be a very tempting target for your puppy's teeth, so you will want to keep them well out their reach.
If you have floor plants, they will need to be moved to a shelf or counter or placed behind a closed door until your curious fur friend grows out of the habit of putting everything in their mouth. Also keep in mind that many common houseplants are poisonous to dogs (discussed in Chapter 16).

**Garage and Yard** – there are obvious as well as subtle dangers that could seriously harm or even kill a Teacup Yorkie puppy, which can often be found in the garage or yard.

Some of these might include antifreeze, gasoline, fertilizers, rat, mice, snail and slug poison, weed killer, paint, cleaners and solvents, grass seed, bark mulch and various insecticides.

If you are storing any of these toxic substances in your garage or garden shed, make certain that you keep all such products inside a locked cabinet, or stored on high shelves that your puppy will not be able to reach. Even better, choose not to use toxic chemicals anywhere in your home or yard.

## 12. Puppy Hazard Home Inspection

Every conscientious puppy guardian needs to take a serious look around the home not just from the human eye level, but also from the eye level of a Teacup Yorkie puppy.

This means literally crawling around your floors. This can be a fun exercise to ask your children to help you with.

Your puppy has a much lower vantage point than you do when standing, therefore, there may be items in your environment that could potentially be harmful to a Teacup Yorkie puppy that a human might not notice unless you get down on the floor and take a really good look.

## 13. First Weeks With Your Puppy

**a) The First Night**

Before you go to the breeder's to pick up your new Teacup Yorkie puppy, vacuum your floors, including all the dust bunnies under the bed.

Do a last minute check of every room to make sure that everything that could be a puppy hazard is carefully tucked away out of sight and that nothing is left on the floor or low down on shelves where a curious puppy might get into trouble.

Close most of the doors inside your home, so that there are just one or two rooms that the puppy will have access to.

You have already been shopping and have everything you need, so get out a puppy pee pad and have it at the ready when you bring your new fur friend home.

## Chapter 8: Choosing the Right Dog

Also have your soft bed(s) in an area where you will be spending most of your time and where your puppy can easily find them.

If you have already purchased a soft toy, take the toy with you when you go to pick up your puppy.

**NOTE**: take either your hard-sided kennel or your soft-sided "Sherpa" travel bag (lined with pee pads) with you when going to bring your new Teacup Yorkie puppy home, and make sure that it is securely fastened to the seat of your vehicle with the seatbelt restraint system.

Even though you will be tempted to hold your new Teacup Yorkie puppy in your lap on the drive home, this is a very dangerous place for them to be, in case of an accident.

Place them inside their kennel or bag, which will be lined with soft towels and perhaps even a warm towel wrapped hot water bottle (and a pee pad), and close the door.

If you have a friend who can drive for you, sit beside your puppy in the back seat, and if they cry on the way home, remind them that they are not alone with your soft, soothing voice.

Before bringing your new Teacup Yorkie puppy inside your home, take them to the place where you want them to relieve themselves and try to wait it out long enough for them to at least go pee.

Then bring them inside your home and introduce them to the area where their food and water bowls will be kept, in case they are hungry or thirsty.

Let your puppy wander around sniffing and checking out their new surroundings and encourage them to follow you wherever you go.

## Chapter 8: Choosing the Right Dog

Show them where the puppy pee pad is located and place it near the door where you will exit to take them outside to go potty. Many pee pads are scented to encourage a puppy to pee, and if they do, happily praise them.

Show them where their hard-sided kennel is (in your bedroom) and put them inside with the door open while you sit on the floor in front and quietly encourage them to relax inside their kennel.

Depending on the time of day when you bring your new Teacup Yorkie puppy home for the first time, practice this kennel exercise several times throughout the day, and if they will take a little treat each time you encourage them to go inside their kennel, this will help to further encourage the behavior of them wanting to go inside.

After they have had their evening meal, take them outside approximately 20 minutes later to go to the bathroom, and when they do, make sure you are very enthusiastic with your praise and perhaps even give a little treat.

So far your Teacup Yorkie puppy has only been allowed in several rooms of your home, as you have kept the other doors closed, so keep it this way for the first few days.

Before it's time for bed, again take your puppy outside for a very short walk to the same place where they last went potty and make sure that they go pee before bringing them back inside.

Before bed, prepare your Teacup Yorkie puppy's hot water bottle and wrap it in a towel so that it will not be too hot for them, and place it inside their hard-sided kennel (in your bedroom).

Turn the lights down low and invite your puppy to go inside their kennel and if they seem interested, perhaps give them a soft toy to have inside with them. Let them walk into the kennel under their own steam and when they do, give them a little treat (if they are interested) and encourage them to snuggle down to sleep while you are sitting on the floor in front of the kennel.

Once they have settled down inside their kennel, close the door, go to your bed and turn all the lights off. It may help your puppy to sleep during their first night home, if you can play quiet, soothing music in the background.

If they start to cry or whine, stay calm and have compassion because this is the first time in their young life when they do not have the comfort of their mother or their litter mates.

Do not let them out of their kennel if they are crying, but rather, simply reassure them with your calm voice that they are not alone until they fall asleep.

**TIP**: if your bed is wide enough to accommodate your puppy's kennel, it may help them to fall asleep for the first few nights in their new kennel, if you have it beside you on top of the bed, so that you are closer to them. If there is any danger of the kennel falling off the bed during the night, do NOT do this as you will traumatize your puppy and make them afraid of their kennel.

## b) The First Week

During the first week, you and your new Teacup Yorkie puppy will be getting settled into your new routine, which will involve you getting used to your puppy's needs as they also get used to your usual schedule.

Be as consistent as possible with your waking and sleeping routine, getting up and going to bed at the same time each day, so that it will be easier for your puppy to get into the flow and routine of their new life.

First thing in the morning, remove your puppy from their kennel and take them immediately outside to relieve themselves at the place where they last went pee.

## Chapter 8: Choosing the Right Dog

At this time, if you are teaching them to ring a doorbell to go outside, let them ring the bell before you go out the door with them, whether you are carrying them, or whether they are walking out the door on their own.

**NOTE**: during the first week, you may want to carry your puppy outside first thing in the morning as they may not be able to hold it for very long once waking up.

When you bring them back inside, you can let them follow you so they get used to their new leash and/or harness arrangement.

Be very careful not to drag your puppy if they stop or pull back on the leash.

**TIP**: if they refuse to walk on the leash, just hold the tension toward you (without pulling) while encouraging them to walk toward you, until they start to move forward again.
Now it will be time for their first feed of the day, and after they have finished eating, keep an eye on the clock, because you will want to take them outside to relieve themselves in about 20 minutes.

When your puppy is not eating or napping, they will be wanting to explore and have little play sessions with you and these times will help you bond with your puppy more and more each day.

As their new guardian, it will be your responsibility to keep a close eye on them throughout the day, so that you can notice when they need to relieve themselves and either take them to their pee pad or take them outside.

You will also need to make sure that they are eating and drinking enough throughout the day, so set regular feeding times at least three times a day.

Also set specific times in the day when you will take your puppy out for a little walk on leash and harness, so that they are not only going outside when they need to relieve themselves, but they are also learning to explore their new neighborhood with you beside them.

When your Teacup Yorkie puppy is still very young, you will not want to walk for a long time as they will get tired easily, so keep your walks to no more than 15 or 20 minutes during your first week and if they seem tired or cold, pick them up and carry them home.

## 14. Common Mistakes to Avoid

### a) Sleeping in Your Bed

Many of us humans make the mistake of allowing a crying puppy to sleep with us in our in bed, and while this may help to calm and comfort a new puppy, it will set a dangerous precedent that can result in behavioral problems later in their life.
As well, a sleeping human body can easily crush a Teacup Yorkie puppy.

As much as it may pull on your heart strings to hear your new Teacup Yorkie puppy crying the first couple of night in their kennel, a little tough love at the beginning will keep them safe while helping them to learn to both love and respect you as their leader.

### b) Picking Them Up at the Wrong Time

Never pick your puppy up if they display nervousness, fear or aggression (such as growling) toward an object, person or other pet, because this will be rewarding them for unbalanced behavior.

Instead, your puppy needs to be gently corrected by you, with firm and calm energy so that they learn not to react with fear or aggression.

## Chapter 8: Choosing the Right Dog

### c) Armpit Alligators

It is important to be aware that many guardians get into the bad habit of carrying a small dog far too much. They need to be on the ground and walking on their own so that they do not become overly confident because a dog that is carried by their guardian is literally being placed in the *"top dog"* position.

Humans who constantly carry small dogs around rather than allowing them to walk on their own can often inadvertently create what I refer to as an *"armpit alligator"* situation.

While the Teacup Yorkie is usually tolerant of other people and pets, it is possible to allow them to become protective or possessive of *"their"* humans. In this case, they may become snappy whenever another human or dog approaches.

When a dog has been allowed to become possessive of it's guardian who carries it everywhere, when another adult, child or dog sees the cute little dog and approaches to say hello, the cute little dog who has been inadvertently trained to believe that it is the boss, may then lunge, snap and/or growl.

### d) Playing Too Hard or Too Long

Many humans play too hard or allow their children to play too long or too roughly with a young puppy.

You need to remember that a young puppy tires very easily and especially during the critical growing phases of their young life, they need their rest. In the case of a teacup sized Yorkie, they will be that much more fragile, especially when still growing puppies.

### e) Hand Play

Always discourage your Teacup Yorkie puppy from chewing or biting your hands, or any part of your body for that matter.

*Chapter 8: Choosing the Right Dog*

If you allow them to do this when they are puppies, they will want to continue to do so when they have strong jaws and adult teeth and this is not acceptable behavior for any breed of dog.

Do not get into the habit of playing the *"hand"* game, where you rough up the puppy and slide them across the floor with your hands, because this will teach your puppy that your hands are playthings.

When your puppy is teething, they will naturally want to chew on everything within reach, and this will include you. As cute as you might think it is, this is not an acceptable behavior and you need to gently, but firmly, discourage the habit.

A light flick with a finger on the end of a puppy nose, combined with a firm "NO" when they are trying to bite human fingers will discourage them from this activity.

**f) Not Getting Used to Grooming**

Not taking the time to get your Teacup Yorkie used to a regular grooming routine, including bathing, brushing, toenail clipping and teeth brushing can lead to a lifetime of trauma for both human and dog every time these procedures must be performed.

Set aside a few minutes each day for your grooming routine and start right from the first day you bring them home.

**NOTE**: get your Teacup Yorkie used to being up high, on a table or countertop when you are grooming them, because when it comes time for a full grooming session, then they will not be stressed by being placed on a grooming table.

**g) Free Feeding**

Free feeding means to keep food in your puppy's bowl 24/7 so that they can eat any time of the day or night, whenever they feel like it.

## Chapter 8: Choosing the Right Dog

While free feeding a young puppy can be a good idea until they are about four or five months old, many guardians of smaller breed dogs often get into the bad habit of allowing their adult dogs to continue to eat food any time they want, by leaving food out 24/7.

This can be a serious mistake, because although you need to ensure that your puppy is eating enough throughout the day, your Teacup Yorkie needs to know that you are absolutely in control of their food.

If your Teacup Yorkie does not associate the food they eat with you, they may become picky eaters or think that they are the boss, which can lead to other behavioral issues later in life.

**h) Treating Them Like Fur Children**

Do not get into the bad habit of treating your Teacup Yorkie like a small fur human, because even though they may try their best to please you, and their doggy smarts could help them to succeed in most instances, not honoring them for the amazing dog they are will only cause them confusion that could lead to behavioral problems.

Remember that the one thing that your Teacup Yorkie is the absolute best at is being a dog.

A well-balanced Teacup Yorkie thrives on rules and boundaries, and when they understand that there is no question that you are their leader and they are your follower, they will live a contented, happy and stress-free life.

**i) Distraction and Replacement**

When your puppy tries to chew on your hand, foot, or your clothing, or anything else that is not fair game, you need to firmly and calmly tell them "No", and then distract them by replacing what they are not supposed to be chewing with their chew toy.

Make sure that you happily praise them every time they choose the toy to chew on.

If the puppy persists in chewing on you, remove yourself from the equation by getting up and walking away. If they are really persistent, put them inside their kennel with a favorite chew toy until they calm down.

Always praise your puppy when they stop inappropriate behavior so that they begin to understand what they can and cannot do.

## 15. Bonding With Your Dog

You will begin bonding with your Teacup Yorkie puppy from the very first moment you bring them home from the breeders.

This is the time when your puppy will be the most upset and nervous, as they will no longer have the guidance, warmth and comfort of their mother or their other littermates, and you will need to take on the role of being your new puppy's center of attention.

Be patient, kind and gentle with them as they are learning you are now their new center of the universe.

Your daily interaction with your puppy during play sessions and especially your disciplined exercises, including going for walks on leash, and teaching commands and tricks, will all be wonderful bonding opportunities. Never make the mistake of thinking that *"bonding"* with your new puppy can only happen if you are playing or cuddling together, because the very best bonding happens when you are kindly teaching rules and boundaries, and this intelligent puppy will be most eager to learn.

### What Does the Wag Mean?

It can be a mistake to automatically assume that if a dog is wagging their tail that they are happy and friendly.

## Chapter 8: Choosing the Right Dog

When determining a dog's true intent or demeanor, you need to take into consideration the entire dog because it is entirely possible that a dog can be wagging it's tail just before it decides to take an aggressive lunge toward you.

More important in determining the emotional state of a dog is the height or positioning of the their tail.

For instance, a tail that is held parallel to the dog's back usually suggests that the dog is feeling relaxed, whereas, if the tail is held stiffly vertical, this usually means that the dog is feeling aggressive or dominant.

A tail held much lower can mean that the dog is feeling stressed, afraid, submissive or unwell and if the tail is tucked underneath the dog's body, this is most often a sign that the dog is feeling fearful and threatened by another dog or person.

Paying attention to your dog's tail can help you to know when you need to step in and make some space between your dog and another more dominant dog.

Of course, different breeds naturally carry their tails at different heights, so you will need to take this into consideration when studying your dog's tail so that you get used to their particular signals.

As well, the speed the tail is moving will also give you an idea of the mental state of the dog because the speed of the wag usually indicates how excited a dog may be.

For instance, a slow, slightly swinging wag can often mean that the dog is tentative about greeting another dog, and this is more of a questioning type of wag, whereas a fast moving tail held high can mean that a dog is about to challenge or threaten another less dominant dog.

*Chapter 8: Choosing the Right Dog*

A dog that was wagging it's tail and then suddenly stops when they see your Teacup Yorkie may be an indication that they have just switched into *"prey"* mode and are about to pounce on your tiny dog.

Interestingly, two veterinarians at the University of Bari and a neuroscientist at the University of Trieste, in Italy, published a paper in which their research outlined that dogs' tails wagged more to their right side when they had positive feelings about a person or situation, and more to the left side when they were feeling negative.

While certainly a dog's tail can help us humans to understand how our dogs might be feeling, there are many other factors to take into consideration when determining your dog's state of mind.

# Chapter 9: Health Problems

Generally speaking, while a Yorkie puppy will be susceptible to any type of health conditions that affect either of their parents.

Yorkshire Terriers are generally quite healthy little dogs, however, any breed can suffer from health problems for a variety of reasons, some of which may be genetic, some of which may result from those Yorkies who are bred to be especially small, and some that may be prevented by educating yourself about common issues that may occur during the life of your pet.

## 1. Common Issues

Although most traditional sized Yorkshire Terriers will probably stay fairly healthy most of their life, and every dog can suffer from health problems, the tiny Teacup Yorkie may have more health problems.

However, if you educate yourself about some of the problems that may afflict the Yorkshire Terrier, this will be your best prevention, because you will be able to recognize potential symptoms and problems and get your dog the right treatment more quickly.

Many conditions can be treated successfully when recognized early on in the dog's life.

As with most purebred dogs, a Yorkshire Terrier will be predisposed to certain health conditions, which doesn't mean that your dog, or every dog of this breed will have these conditions, and in fact, many never suffer from any of these noted health problems or illnesses, especially if your dog comes from a reputable breeder.

## 2. Congenital Defects

Congenital defects refer to abnormalities of the body that are present when the puppy is born. These types of defects may involve any part of the puppy's body or any system or organ within the puppy's body.

Some congenital defects can be slight or minor and may naturally resolve themselves as the puppy grows, while others defects can cause or prevent the normal development and function of the puppy, even to the point of causing early death.

Some congenital defects can be very obvious at birth, while many others may remain hidden for months, years or even for the entire lifetime of the dog.

Congenital defects can occur at any time during the early stages of the embryo or fetus when the majority of organ systems are developing, which can cause serious defects, or later on during the second half of pregnancy, which may be less severe.

Defects can occur for no understandable or known reason, they can be inherited from the puppy's parents, they might even be caused by adverse environmental factors, or a combination of any of these.

Although what causes congenital defects is largely unknown, it is possible that environmental circumstances present during the female dog's pregnancy may lead to certain defects.

For instance, trauma or temperature extremes (hot or cold) may cause problems in fetal development that could include cleft palates, dwarfism, extra vertebrae, hydrocephalus (water on the brain) polydactylism (extra toes), or pectus excavatum (intrusion of the breastbone into the thoracic cavity.

Should a mother dog be exposed to certain infections or chemicals in the environment during her pregnancy, this can increase the risk of her puppies being born with birth defects.

For instance, a widely used drug, used to treat ringworm is an example of a medication used to cure ringworm that can cause cleft palate in the growing fetus.

Also, some congenital defects that are specific to particular breeds are a result of exaggerated characteristic breed features, such as tracheal collapse, which is commonly seen in short-nosed breeds of dogs, including the Yorkshire Terrier.

Certain genetic predispositions have been found to occur in the Yorkie breed. The more common congenital defects include:

## a) Distichiasis

This is a condition that causes eye irritation (tearing, squinting, inflammation ulcers or abrasions to the cornea) where the eyelashes grow from an abnormal area, usually from the tear duct at the edge of the eyelid. These errant eyelashes may be removed with electrolysis or surgery.

## b) Hydrocephalus

This is water on the brain, which can be caused by overproduction of spinal fluid and congenitally this defect is more likely to occur in small and brachycephalic (short nosed) dogs, such as the Yorkie.

A tumor in the eye may also be the cause of water on the brain. In Yorkshire Terriers, it is an inherited disease that usually becomes apparent at a few weeks of age up to about a year.

Symptoms may include lack of bladder or bowel control, sleepiness, excess vocalization, blindness, seizures, large dome-shaped head, crossed eyes, gait abnormalities, difficulty breathing, arching of the head, extension of all four legs, and coma. Prognosis and treatment of this disease can vastly vary, with results ranging from good to poor, depending on the severity.

## c) Hypoglycemia

This is the medical term for low blood sugar, which is caused when a puppy or very small dog fasts too long between meals and is usually seen in puppies between the ages of 5 and 16 weeks. The smaller the Yorkshire Terrier puppy, the more they are prone to hypoglycemia because their lack of muscle mass makes it difficult to store glucose and regulate their blood sugar.

A puppy suffering from low blood sugar will become drowsy, glassy-eyed, listless, shaky and uncoordinated because the brain relies upon sugar to in order to function properly.

Another indication will be gums that are very pale or grey in color and at this time the puppy may require force-feeding and injections of fluids because the puppy may also be dehydrated. Left untreated, the consequences of low blood sugar are very serious as the puppy may have a seizure or go into a coma. A puppy or dog displaying these symptoms should be given sugar in the form of corn syrup or honey and immediate veterinary treatment because the longer the brain is starved of sugar, the higher the chance that the puppy will suffer from permanent brain damage or even death.

## d) Hypoplasia of Dens

This condition, which affects the formation of the second cervical vertebra, can cause spinal cord damage at any age, with resulting signs ranging from neck pain to four-limb paralysis (quadriplegia). However, with proper care, it is still possible for some dogs with this condition to recover to the point where they can walk again.

## e) Legg-Calve-Perthes Syndrome

This condition causes the top of the thighbone (the femur) to degenerate as a result of poor or inadequate circulation around the hip joint.

When blood flow to this area is reduced, the head of the femur eventually collapses and dies, which then causes the cartilage coating surrounding the area to become dry, cracked and deformed.

This syndrome usually occurs before the dog reaches one year old (between 5 and 8 months of age) with indications showing themselves as pain, limping or lameness and treatment requires surgery to remove the affected area of the bone.

After surgery, thankfully the dog will have normal use of the affected leg, although it will be left shorter than the other three legs.

## f) Luxating Patella

This slipping kneecap condition is a common defect in Yorkshire Terriers and other small dogs, although accidentally falling or jumping from a height may also cause the problem.

Often you will see a dog with this problem appear to be skipping down the road as they occasionally life one rear leg when the kneecap slips out of the patellar groove and the leg locks up. Many dogs live a perfectly normal life without any intervention, while more serious cases may require surgery.

## g) Portosystemic Shunt

This is a serious congenital malformation of the portal vein that brings blood to the liver for cleansing and if not treated, can lead to seizures, blindness, coma and death. I

When a dog has this condition, some of the dog's blood will bypass the liver, which means that this blood will not be cleansed of harmful toxins before it returns to poison the heart and other vital organs.

A Yorkshire Terrier with this condition may display multiple symptoms, including poor appetite, vomiting, diarrhea, stunted growth, poor coordination, weak muscles, difficulty learning and behavioral problems.

## h) Progressive Retinal Atrophy (PRA)

PRA is an inherited, degenerative disease of the retina of the eye that is incurable.

The first symptom will be night blindness, followed by a gradual loss of daytime vision, and eventual total blindness.

The best opportunity for avoiding this condition is to ensure that you purchase your Yorkshire Terrier only through a qualified, reputable breeder who takes all necessary precautions to breed only dogs who are known to be free from these conditions and less likely to pass them on to litters of puppies.

## i) Tracheal Collapse

Tracheal collapse is also called *"Brachycephalic Airway Syndrome"* and occurs in many small or toy dog breeds, caused by a weakening of the walls of the trachea. This condition can worsen with age.

The first time you witness the cough that is some call *"goose honking"*, you will likely be quite alarmed, thinking your dog is dying as he is trying to breathe through a partially collapsed trachea. Thankfully, these episodes are usually very short in duration, lasting only a few seconds.

Sometimes you can help your dog to regain full breathing by rubbing the nose, which causes them to open their mouths and relax the trachea. Also holding the dog's ribs and carefully giving a slight, sharp squeeze to encourage airflow can be effective. Oftentimes the condition presents itself when the dog becomes too excited over food or play with other dogs or during warmer weather.

Many dogs live normal lives without any intervention, however, if the condition becomes severe, sometimes it can be surgically corrected.

## j) Bladder Stones

Middle-aged or older Yorkshire Terriers tend to suffer from bladder stones and signs to be aware of with this condition include blood in the urine and difficulty going to the bathroom.

## k) Heart Disease

Yorkies can be prone to heart disease, especially with valves that may fail to close properly.

If a dog has a heart valve problem, blood will flow back into the chamber, which can cause the chamber to enlarge in size, which then can cause other problems, such as blood flowing back into the lungs, an irregular heartbeat or a constricted windpipe.

Symptoms may include tiredness, intolerance to exercise, poor appetite, weight loss, persistent cough, breathing problems and fainting or collapsing episodes.

A heart valve condition usually presents itself when the dog is older, and is usually only discovered during a routine examination, when a veterinarian hears a heart murmur, and unfortunately, treatment will not prolong the life of the dog.

## l) Retained Milk Teeth

Many times smaller breeds, like the Yorkie, do not naturally lose their puppy or milk teeth without help from a licensed veterinarian.
Keep a close watch on your puppy's teeth around 4 to 8 months of age when they begin to lose their baby teeth, to make certain that

*Chapter 9: Health Problems*

the baby teeth have fallen out and that the adult teeth have adequate space to grown in.

If your puppy has not naturally lost their baby teeth, they will need to be pulled, in order to allow room for the adult teeth to grow in.

## m) Canine Hypothyroidism

A Yorkie dog or puppy suffering from hypothyroidism (an under active thyroid), has a disorder of the thyroid gland.

They may be experiencing hair loss, a coat that has lost its shine, tiredness, weight gain, extreme intolerance to cold weather and chronic skin problems.

Although hypothyroidism is a permanent problem, it can be effectively treated when carefully monitored by physical examination, which includes blood testing, urinalysis, biochemistry profile and endocrine testing.

Once it has been discovered that your dog is suffering from canine hypothyroidism, they will require monitoring and ongoing medication adjustment.

The thyroid regulates the dog's metabolic rate and a dog suffering from this disorder that receives thyroid hormone replacement treatment will be able to maintain good health and a normal life span well into their old age. Reputable Yorkshire Terrier breeders will have had their breeding dogs regularly screened for this problem and if found positive will cease breeding these dogs because the problem will be passed on to the puppies.

## n) Cryptorchidism

This common birth defect is a condition is also referred to as *"retained testicles"* and in the male Yorkshire Terrier puppy, sometimes one or both of the testicles will not have descended into the scrotum.

This condition rarely occurs beyond six months of age, because normally the testes should have descended into the scrotum area when the puppy is around two months of age.

When one or both testes do not descend into the scrotum, this means that they remain somewhere in the lower part of the puppy's body. They may be felt in the inguinal canal, which is a passage in the groin area that conveys the spermatic cord to the testes. If it is deeper in the abdomen then ultrasound testing will be the best option in order to determine the size and location.

Toy breeds, such as the Teacup Yorkshire Terrier, are at significantly higher risk for this condition and interestingly, the right testis fails to descend into the scrotum twice as often as the left side.

It is not advised to leave an undescended testicle in the body of the puppy as this could result in an increased risk of cancer.

Treatment for the condition involves neutering, and in most cases, unless the puppy is being used for breeding purposes, this will not be a problem because they will be neutered anyway.

## o) Delicate Digestive Symptoms

The Yorkie breed can often suffer from a delicate digestive system, with the resultant vomiting or diarrhea from consuming foods not usually part of their regular diet.

This is not a dog that should be fed human food, various table scraps or anything outside of its normal canine feeding routine.

If your Yorkie starts to throw up or displays unusual eating or eliminating problems, make sure that you check for changes in their diet.

Sudden changes in diet, their environment or their usual daily routine can cause stomach problems, including excessive gas, stomach pains and diarrhea.

If you want to change their food, make sure that you do this very slowly, over a couple of weeks, by mixing in a small amount of the new food with the old, and then gradually increasing the new food until you have them totally switched over.

The Yorkshire Terrier also should not be given human food or a wide variety of dog treats and you need to be careful to keep any sort of tempting items far out of their reach because they are naturally keen hunters who will quickly ferret out and eat food that they should not have access to.

Once you find a premium brand of food that agrees with your Yorkie, it's best not to upset their delicate balance by continually introducing new foods.

## p) Intolerance to Anesthesia

As a result of the small size of the Yorkshire Terrier, and even more so in the abnormally small *"teacup"* varieties, this means that they will usually have a poor tolerance to anesthesia.

There is much discussion concerning the dangers of anesthesia with small dogs, and understandably, the smaller the dog, the higher the risk when administering anesthesia, or any kind of drug for that matter.

It's especially important that toy breed sizes, like the Yorkshire Terrier, are carefully weighed so that the appropriate dose and type of anesthetic is given during surgery based on their small size.

As well, while careful monitoring of blood pressure and blood glucose levels during surgical procedures is crucial for all canine patients, this is particularly so for the tiny ones who tend to have

## Chapter 9: Health Problems

lower body temperatures and low blood sugar (hypoglycemia).

If you are concerned about neutering or spaying your Yorkshire Terrier, be sure to ask your veterinarian plenty of questions so that you are assured that they are up to speed with all the latest techniques that can reduce risk for smaller dogs.

To ensure that the puppy you may be considering is as healthy as possible, always ask questions about whether the parents of a particular puppy have been screened and are free from the types of health problems that may be inherent in the breed.

While a Teacup Yorkie is a much more fragile dog than a standard sized Yorkie, this toy breed is generally quite healthy and when from healthy breeding stock and well cared for can enjoy an average life expectancy of approximately 15 years, with some living even longer.

To ensure that the puppy you may be considering is as healthy as possible, always ask questions about whether the parents of a particular puppy have been screened and are free from the types of health problems that may be inherent in either breed.

## 3. Fragility

Fragility will always be an issue to take into consideration when considering a smaller, Teacup Yorkie whose bones can easily be broken.

## Chapter 9: Health Problems

Many people do not realize how incredibly fragile a toy breed can be, let alone one that is "teacup" sized, or that without taking proper care, you can seriously injure or kill a small Yorkie by stepping on them or by accidentally sitting on them.

As well, a small Yorkie can break bones, seriously injure or even kill itself by fearlessly leaping from your arms or off the back of your sofa, and a larger dog with a high prey drive can quickly grab a small Yorkie and break his neck with one quick shake.

If you are determined to own a smaller sized Yorkie, this will mean that you must be constantly vigilant and keep your dog under supervision and surveillance so that you are aware of everything that is happening around your dog and can avoid any sort of harm that may befall them, which can also come from the air, as large birds of prey can easily carry off a small Yorkie.

Small Yorkies with fearless attitudes should always be kept on leash because they may place themselves into all sorts of circumstances whereby they could easily be injured when they are not under your complete control.

Also, very small Yorkies would NOT be suitable pets for young children, who may accidentally hurt them, or drop them.

Children are usually loud, fast moving, boisterous and oftentimes clumsy, which is a combination for danger around a small dog that might suffer all manner of injuries at the hands of a young child that meant well.

Further, most small dogs will feel overwhelmed by the loud, shrill voices and quick movements that young children can't help making with the result being that the dog may experience stress, fear and even defensive biting while it tries to defend itself from what it may believe to be a threat.

## 4. Allergies

One of the most common complaints discussed at the veterinarian's office when they see dogs scratching and chewing at themselves is possible allergies.

Unlike us humans, who react to allergies with nasal symptoms, when our dogs are suffering from allergies they will typically present itchy skin or ear problems.

**a) Environmental**

Allergies are usually first noticed because your Teacup Yorkie is scratching, itching, biting, licking or chewing at their skin or paws.

Just like us humans, our dogs can develop allergies to dust, chemicals, grass, mold, pollen, car exhaust, cigarette smoke, and flea and tick preparations, as well as allergies to materials, such as wool or cotton, and chemicals found in washing soap or chemicals found in cleaning products you use around your home.

Symptoms are usually seen on the stomach, inside of the legs, and at the tail or paws.

Since most allergies are seasonal, our dogs will be more affected in the spring or fall. Airborne irritants inhaled by your Teacup Yorkie, may result in coughing, sneezing or watery eyes.

If you think that your dog may have come in contact with an environmental irritant, the best thing you can do for your dog is give them a cleansing bath, with the proper canine shampoo, followed by canine conditioner.

Remember that a Teacup Yorkie is especially close to the ground, and the longer their hair, the more they resemble a duster who attracts everything they come into contact with.

## b) Junk Food

*"True"* food allergies usually account for only about 10% of allergy problems in our canine friends.

For instance, itching, chewing and chronic ear infections are not actually caused by food allergies, but rather are the result of a suppressed immune system, which is caused by eating a low quality diet.

These types of food allergies can oftentimes be completely resolved by changing your Teacup Yorkie's diet to a high quality food that is more easily digested. Proper nutrition is the easiest way to prevent any food allergies.

Many dog food products contain corn, wheat and soybeans, which are common allergens. Usually it is the gluten in these foods that cause the allergic reaction.

Visit your local pet food store and educate yourself or talk with a knowledgeable representative because there's no excuse for feeding your dog a junk food diet when there are so many healthy choices now available that will help your canine companion live a long and healthy life.

# Chapter 10: Daily Feeding and Care

## 1. Feeding Puppies

For growing puppies, a general feeding rule of thumb is to feed 10% of the puppy's present body weight or between 2% and 3% of their projected adult weight each day.

Keep in mind that high energy puppies will require extra protein to help them grow and develop into healthy adult dogs, especially during their first two years of life.

There are now many foods on the market that are formulated for all stages of a dog's life (including the puppy stage), so whether you choose one of these foods or a food specially formulated for puppies, they will need to be fed smaller meals more frequently throughout the day (3 or 4 times), until they are at least one year of age.

**NOTE**: choose quality sources of meat protein for healthy puppies and dogs, including beef, buffalo, chicken, duck, fish, hare, lamb, ostrich, pork, rabbit, turkey, venison, or any other source of wild meaty protein.

## 2. Feeding Adults

An adult dog will generally need to be fed between 2% and 3% of their body weight each day. Read the labels and avoid foods that

## Chapter 10: Daily Feeding and Care

contain a high amount of grains and other fillers. Choose foods that list high quality meat protein as the main ingredient.

**TIP:** grated parmesan cheese sprinkled on a Teacup Yorkie's dinner will help to stop picky eaters from ignoring their food. To get the cheese to stick to the kibble, first mix a small amount of olive oil into the kibble, and then sprinkle with finely grated Parmesan cheese.

## 3. Treats

Since the creation of the first dog treat over 150 years ago the myriad of choices available on every pet store, feed store and grocery store shelf almost outnumbers those looking forward to eating them.

Today's treats are not just for making us guilty humans feel better because it makes us happy to give our fur friends something they really enjoy because today's treats are also designed to actually improve our dog's health.

Some of us humans treat our dogs, just because, others use treats for training purposes, others for health, while still others treat for a combination of reasons.

Whatever reason you choose to give treats to your Teacup Yorkie, keep in mind that if we treat our dogs too often throughout the day, we may create a picky eater who will no longer want to eat their regular meals.

As well, if the treats we are giving are high calorie, we may be putting our dog's health in jeopardy by allowing them to become overweight.

**TIP:** an interesting article written by Jonathan O'Callaghan, recently published on June 12, 2014 in the Daily Mail, indicates that researchers in Sweden have discovered that dogs were visibly happier when they had to earn their treats as a reward for completing a task, rather than just being given a treat for looking cute.

Apparently, just like us humans get that happy "eureka" moment when we finally solve a problem, so do our canine counterparts.

If you've been treating your dog for no other reason that just because they looked expectantly at the cookie jar, perhaps now is the time to change your human habits and ask your dog to perform a trick or have to search for a hidden treat, so that your dog can also feel that emotional excitement of being rewarded for accomplishing a task.

## 4. Treats to Avoid

### a) Rawhide

Rawhide is soaked in an ash/lye solution to remove every particle of meat, fat and hair and then further soaked in bleach to remove remaining traces of the ash/lye solution. Now that the product is no longer food, it no longer has to comply with food regulations.

While the hide is still wet it is shaped into rawhide chews, and upon drying it shrinks to approximately 1/4 of its original size.

Further, arsenic based products are often used as preservatives, and antibiotics and insecticides are added to kill bacteria that also fight against good bacteria in your dog's intestines.

The collagen fibers in the rawhide make it very tough and long lasting which makes this chew a popular choice for humans to give to their dogs because it satisfies the dog's natural urge to chew while providing many hours of quiet entertainment.

Sadly, when a dog chews a rawhide treat, they ingest many harsh chemicals and when your dog swallows a piece of rawhide, that piece now can swell up to four times its size inside your dog's stomach, which can cause anything from mild to severe gastric blockages that could become life threatening and require surgery.

**b) Pig Ears**

These treats are actually the ears of pigs, and while most dogs will eagerly devour them, they are extremely high in fat, which can cause stomach upsets, vomiting and diarrhea for many dogs.

Pig ears are often processed and preserved with unhealthy chemicals that discerning dog guardians will not want to feed their dogs.

As well, the ears are often quite thin and crispy and when the dog chews them pieces can break off, like chips, and can easily become stuck in a dog's throat.

While pig ears are generally not considered to be a healthy treat choice for any dog, they should be especially avoided for any dog that may be at risk of being overweight.

**c) Hoof Treats**

Many humans give cow, horse and pig hooves to their dogs as treats because they consider them to be *"natural"*.

The truth is that after processing these *"treats"* they retain little, if any, of their *"natural"* qualities.

Hoof treats are processed with harsh preservatives, including insecticides, lead, bleach, arsenic based products, and antibiotics to kill bacteria, that can also harm the good bacteria in your dog's intestines, and if all bacteria is not killed in these meat based products before feeding them to your dog, they could also suffer from Salmonella poisoning.

Hooves can also cause chipping or breaking of your dog's teeth as well as perforation or blockages in your dog's intestines.

## 5. Healthy Treats

### a) Hard Treats

There are so many choices of hard, or crunchy treats available that come in many varieties of shapes, sizes and flavors, that you may have a difficult time choosing.

If your Teacup Yorkie will eat them, hard treats will help to keep their teeth cleaner.

Whatever you do choose, be certain to read the labels and make sure that the ingredients are high quality and appropriately sized for your Teacup Yorkie friend.

### b) Soft Treats

Soft, chewy treats are also available in endless varieties and flavors, suitable for all the different needs of our fur friends and are often used for training purposes as they have a stronger smell.

### c) Dental Treats

Dental treats or chews are designed with the specific purpose of helping your Teacup Yorkie to maintain healthy teeth and gums.

They usually require intensive chewing and are often shaped with high ridges and bumps to exercise the jaw and massage gums while removing plaque build-up near the gum line.

### d) Freeze-Dried and Jerky Treats

Freeze-dried and jerky treats offer a tasty morsel most dogs find

*Chapter 10: Daily Feeding and Care*

irresistible as they are usually made of simple, meaty ingredients, such as liver, poultry and seafood.

These treats are usually lightweight and easy to carry around, which means they can also be great as training treats.

**e) Human Food Treats**

You will want to be very careful when feeding human foods to dogs as treats, because many of our foods contain additives and ingredients that could be toxic and harmful. Be certain to choose simple, fresh foods with minimal or no processing, such as lean meat, poultry or seafood, and even if your Teacup Yorkie will eat anything put in front of them, be aware that many common human foods, such as grapes, raisins, onions and chocolate are poisonous to dogs.

**f) Training Treats**

While any sort of treat can be used as an extra incentive during training sessions, soft treats are often used for training purposes because of their stronger smell and smaller sizes.

Yes, we humans love to treat our dogs, whether for helping to teach the new puppy to go pee outside, teaching the adolescent dog new commands, for trick training, for general good behavior, or for no reason at all, other than that they just gave us the *"look"*.

Generally, the treats you feed your dog should not make up more than approximately 10% of their daily food intake, so make sure the treats you choose are high quality, so that you can help to keep your Teacup Yorkie both happy and healthy.

## 6. Choosing the Right Food

In order to choose the right food for your Teacup Yorkie, first, it's important to understand a little bit about canine physiology and what Mother Nature intended when she created our fur friends.

## Chapter 10: Daily Feeding and Care

More than 230 years ago, in 1785, the English Sportman's dictionary described the best diet for a dog's health in an article entitled *"Dog"*.

This article indicated that the best food for a dog was something called "Greaves", described as "the sediment of melted tallow. It is made into cakes for dogs' food. In Scotland and parts of the US it is called cracklings."

Out of the meager beginning of the first commercially made dog food has sprung a massively lucrative and vastly confusing industry that has only recently begun to evolve beyond those early days of feeding our dogs the dregs of human leftovers because it was cheap and convenient for us humans.

Even today, the majority of dog food choices have far more to do with being convenient for humans to store and serve than it does with being a diet truly designed to be a nutritionally balanced, healthy food choice for a canine.

The dog food industry is big business and as such, because there are now almost limitless choices, there is much confusion and endless debate when it comes to answering the question, *"What is the best food for my dog?"*

Educating yourself, by talking to experts and reading everything you can find on the subject, plus taking into consideration several relevant factors, will help to answer the dog food question for you and your dog.

For instance, where you live may dictate what sorts of foods you have access to. Other factors to consider will include the particular requirements of your dog, such as their age, energy and activity levels.

Next will be expense, time and quality. While we all want to give our dogs the best food possible, many humans lead very busy lives and cannot, for instance, prepare their own dog food, but still want to feed a high quality diet that fits within their budget.

However, perhaps most important when choosing an appropriate diet for our dogs, is learning to be more observant of Mother Nature's design and taking a closer look at our dog's teeth, jaws and digestive tract.

While humans are herbivores who derive energy from eating plants, our canine companions are carnivores, which means that they derive their energy and nutrient requirements from eating a diet consisting mainly or exclusively of the flesh of animal tissues (in other words, meat).

## a) The Canine Teeth

The first part of your dog you will want to take a good look at when considering what to feed will be their teeth.

Unlike humans, who are equipped with wide, flat molars for grinding grains, vegetables and other plant-based materials, canine teeth are all pointed because they are designed to rip, shred and tear into animal meat and bone.

## b) The Canine Jaw

Another obvious consideration when choosing an appropriate food source for our fur friends, is the fact that every canine is born equipped with powerful jaws and neck muscles for the specific purpose of being able to pull down and tear apart their hunted prey.
The structure of the jaw of every canine is such that it opens widely to hold large pieces of meat and bone, while the actual mechanics of a dog's jaw permits only vertical (up and down) movement that is designed for crushing.

*Chapter 10: Daily Feeding and Care*

## c) The Canine Digestive Tract

A dog's digestive tract is short and simple and designed to move their natural choice of food (hide, meat and bone) quickly through their systems.

Vegetables and plant matter require more time to break down in the gastrointestinal tract, which in turn, requires a more complex digestive system than the canine body is equipped with.

The canine digestive system is simply unable to break down vegetable matter, which is why whole vegetables look pretty much the same going into your dog as they do coming out the other end.

Given the choice, most dogs would never choose to eat plants or vegetables and fruits over meat, however, we humans continue to feed them a kibble based diet that contains high amounts of vegetables, fruits and grains and low amounts of meat.

Plus, in order to get our dogs to eat fruits, vegetables and grains we usually have to flavor the food with meat or meat by-products.

How much healthier and long lived might our beloved fur friends be if, instead of largely ignoring nature's design for our canine companions, we chose to feed them whole, unprocessed, species-appropriate food?

With many hundreds of dog food brands to choose from, it's no wonder we humans are confused about what to feed our dogs to help them live long and healthy lives.

Following are some suggestions and questions that may help you choose a dog food company that you can feel comfortable with:

- How long have they have been in business?
- Is dog food their main industry?
- Are they dedicated to their brand?

- Are they easily accessible?
- Do they honestly answer your questions?
- Do they have a good Company Safety Standard?
- Do they set higher standards?
- Read the ingredients - where did they come from?
- Are the ingredients something you would eat?
- Are the ingredients farmed locally?
- Was it cooked using standards you would trust?
- Is the company certified under human food or organic guidelines?

Whatever you decide to feed your Teacup Yorkie, keep in mind that, just as too much wheat, other grains and other fillers in our human diet is having detrimental effects on our human health, the same can be very true for our best fur friends.

Our dogs are also suffering from many of the same life threatening diseases that are commonly found in our human society (heart disease, cancer, diabetes, obesity), which all have a direct correlation to eating genetically altered foods that are no longer pure, in favor of a convenient, processed and packaged diet.

## 7. The Raw Diet

While more and more of us humans are coming to the belief that we are killing ourselves and our dogs with processed foods, others believe that there are dangers involved in feeding raw foods to our fur friends.

Those who are raw feeding advocates believe that the ideal diet for their dog is one which would be very similar to what a dog living in the wild would have access to hunting or foraging, and these canine guardians are often opposed to feeding their dog any sort of commercially manufactured pet foods, because they consider them to be poor substitutes.

## Chapter 10: Daily Feeding and Care

On the other hand, those opposed to feeding their dogs a raw or biologically appropriate raw food diet, believe that the risks associated with food-borne illnesses during the handling and feeding of raw meats outweigh the purported benefits.

Interestingly, even though the United States Food and Drug Administration (FDA) states that they do not advocate a raw diet for dogs, they do advise for those who wish to take this route, that following basic hygiene guidelines for handling raw meat can minimize any associated risks.

Further, high pressure pasteurization (HPP), which is high pressure, water based technology for killing bacteria, is USDA-approved for use on organic and natural food products, and is being utilized by many commercial raw pet food manufacturers.

Interestingly, raw meats purchased at your local grocery store contain a much higher level of acceptable bacteria than raw food produced for dogs because the meat purchased for human consumption is supposed to be cooked, which will kill any bacteria that might be present.

This means that canine guardians feeding their dogs a raw food diet can be quite certain that commercially prepared raw foods sold in pet stores will be safer than raw meats purchased in grocery stores.

Many guardians of high energy, working breed dogs will agree that their dogs thrive on a raw or BARF (Biologically Appropriate Raw Food) diet and strongly believe that the potential benefits of feeding a raw dog food diet are many, including:

- Healthy, shiny coats
- Decreased shedding
- Fewer allergy problems
- Healthier skin
- Cleaner teeth

*Chapter 10: Daily Feeding and Care*

- Fresher breath
- Increased energy levels
- Improved digestion
- Smaller stools
- Strengthened immune system
- Increased mobility in arthritic pets
- Increase or improvement in overall health

All dogs, of every size, whether working breed or companion dogs are amazing athletes in their own right, therefore every dog deserves to be fed the best food available.

A raw diet is a direct evolution of what dogs ate before they became our domesticated pets and we turned toward commercially prepared, easy to serve dry dog food that required no special storage or preparation.

The BARF diet is all about feeding our dogs what they are designed to eat by returning them to their wild, evolutionary diet.

## 8. The Dehydrated Diet

Dehydrated dog food comes in both raw meat and cooked meat forms and these foods are usually air dried to reduce moisture to the level where bacterial growth is inhibited.

The appearance of de-hydrated dog food is very similar to dry kibble and the typical feeding methods include adding warm water before serving, which makes this type of diet both healthy for our dogs and convenient for us to serve.

Dehydrated recipes are made from minimally processed fresh whole foods to create a healthy and nutritionally balanced meal that will meet or exceed the dietary requirements of a healthy canine.

Dehydrating removes only the moisture from the fresh ingredients, which usually means that because the food has not already been cooked at a high temperature, more of the overall nutrition is retained.

A de-hydrated diet is a convenient way to feed your dog a nutritious diet because all you have to do is add warm water, and wait five minutes while the food re-hydrates so your Teacup Yorkie can enjoy a warm meal.

## 9. The Kibble Diet

While many canine guardians are starting to take a closer look at the food choices they are making for their furry companions, there is no mistaking that the convenience and relative economy of dry dog food kibble, that had its beginnings in the 1940's, continues to be the most popular pet food choice for most dog friendly humans.

Some 75 years later, the massive pet food industry offers up a confusingly large number of choices with hundreds of different manufacturers and brand names lining the shelves of veterinarian offices, grocery stores and pet food aisles.

While feeding a high quality bagged kibble diet that has been flavored to appeal to dogs and supplemented with vegetables and fruits to appeal to humans, may keep most every Teacup Yorkie companion happy and relatively healthy, you will ultimately need to decide whether this is the best diet for them.

## 10. The Right Bowl

Following is a brief description of the different categories and types of dog bowls that would be appropriate choices for your Teacup Yorkie's particular needs.

**Automatic Watering Bowls**: are standard dog bowls (often made out of plastic) that are attached to a reservoir container, which is

*Chapter 10: Daily Feeding and Care*

designed to keep water constantly available to your dog as long as there is water remaining in the storage compartment.

**Ceramic/Stoneware Bowls**: an excellent choice for those who like options in personality, color and shape.

**Elevated Bowls**: raised dining table dog bowls are a tidy and classy choice that will make your dog's dinner time a more comfortable experience while getting the bowls off the floor.

**No Skid Bowls**: are for dogs that push their bowls across the floor when eating. A non-skid dog bowl will help keep the feed bowl where you put it.

**No Tip Bowls**: are designed to prevent the messy type of doggy eater from flipping over their dinner or water bowls.

**Stainless Steel Bowls**: are as close to indestructible as a bowl can be, plus they are sanitary, easy to clean and water stays cooler for a longer period of time in a stainless bowl.

**Wooden Bowls**: for those humans concerned about stylish home decor, wooden dog bowl dining stations are beautiful pieces of furniture unto themselves that can enhance your home decor.

**Travel Bowls**: are a convenient, practical and handy addition for every canine travel kit.

Consider a space saving, collapsible dog bowl, made out of hygienic, renewable bamboo that comes in fun colors and different sizes, making it perfect for every travel bowl needs.

If you would like to learn more about all the many dog bowl choices available, visit DogBowlForYourDog.com, which is a comprehensive, one-stop website dedicated to explaining the ins and outs of every food bowl imaginable and helping you find the perfect bowl for all your Teacup Yorkie's needs.

*Chapter 10: Daily Feeding and Care*

## 11. Exercise

All of our canine companions are amazing, natural athletes and because of this, they need daily exercise to stay fit, happy and healthy. The highly energetic Teacup Yorkie is no exception to this rule. Every Teacup Yorkie plenty of daily exercise, and will love going for walks or engaging in any manner of canine sport with their guardian several times every day.

As well, taking your Teacup Yorkie for a disciplined walk, where they are on leash and calmly walking beside you without straining on the leash or trying to lead you, will reinforce that you are the boss and they are the follower.

Any type of disciplined exercise you can engage in with your Teacup Yorkie will help to exercise both their body and their intelligent mind and will burn off pent up daily energy reserves so that your Teacup Yorkie will be a happy and contented companion.

If you find that your Teacup Yorkie is being a pest by chewing inappropriate items around the home or being demanding of your time, or especially unruly when visitors come to call, this is likely because they are not being challenged enough or exercised often enough, or long enough each day to drain out their daily pent up energy.

A healthy, adult Teacup Yorkie will thrive when being walked several times each day and will enjoy the challenge of being engaged in other forms of disciplined activity, such as Obedience, Freestyle Dance or Agility.

## 12. Playtime

Every dog needs some regular playtime each day, and this is even more important with an active breed, such as the Teacup Yorkie, who will be your loving, playful, energetic companion.

While every Teacup Yorkie will be different with respect to what types of games they may enjoy, most Yorkie's will enjoy a game of fetch with a ball or chasing a Frisbee, and some may even enjoy swimming to retrieve a stick.

A fun game of *"Search"*, where you ask your Yorkie to "Sit/Stay" while you hide a favorite treat that they then have to find, will appeal to the Yorkie's ancient hunting instincts.

After a disciplined walk with your Yorkie, they will also enjoy being given the opportunity for some off leash freedom to run, play and socialize with other similar sized dogs.

## 13. Daily Grooming

Daily grooming is a must for any healthy Teacup Yorkie.

Get into the routine of spending at least 15 minutes each day brushing or combing your Teacup Yorkie, checking their ears and nails and brushing their teeth.

## 14. Safe Traveling

Far too many canine guardians do nothing to protect their companions when traveling with them inside their vehicles.

According to a 2011 American Automobile Association study, only about 16% of dog owners restrain their pets when riding in a vehicle, and of those who are trying, many are not properly securing their beloved pets.

That leaves 84% of people who let their dogs roam freely about the inside of their vehicles, leaving them at serious risk of being injured or killed in an automobile accident.

For example, when a vehicle traveling at only 30 miles per hour (48.28 kilometers per hour) is involved in an accident, a small, ten pound (4.54 kg), unrestrained dog will be subjected to

## Chapter 10: Daily Feeding and Care

approximately 300 pounds force (136 kilogram-force), which is certainly enough to seriously injure or kill a Teacup Yorkie.

There is no denying that dogs that are not properly restrained become projectiles in any sort of vehicle crash.

As well, many drivers permit their smaller dogs to sit on their lap when driving, which is not only distracting to the driver, but if involved in an accident, the vehicle's airbags will deploy at 300 mph (482.8 kilometers per hour) which can easily snap the neck of a small dog.

**a) Faulty Restraints**

Many dog lovers may be laboring under the misconception that they are doing the right thing by buckling their canine companions into a safety harness because they are unaware that many of these dog harnesses that are supposed to keep furry passengers safe have a 100% failure rate.

Statistics collected by the Center for Pet Safety (CPS) have shown that every popular restraint tested with dog dummies, traveling at a sedate 30 mph (48.28 km/h), not only failed, but also indicated that serious injuries or deaths were highly likely.

Most restraints that were tested in the CPS study allowed dogs to easily become flying projectiles during vehicle accidents because the harnesses were simply not strong enough to keep them in their seats, and in many cases the restraints could actually choke the dog during a crash.

When the MGA Research Corporation carried out a pilot study for The Center for Pet Safety (CPS), in which they tested 12 major brands of pet harnesses, the results indicated a **100% failure rate**.

According to the American Kennel Club, these safety harness tests were carried out using the average weights of the ten most popular breeds of dogs, including the Yorkshire Terrier, the

## Chapter 10: Daily Feeding and Care

German Shepherd, the Golden Retriever, the Beagle, the Bulldog, the Yorkshire Terrier, the Boxer, the Poodle, the Rottweiler and the Poodle.

The founder and chairman of CPS, believes that, *"Saying that these products prevent your pet from becoming a projectile in an accident is a potentially misleading statement."*

Law enforcement agencies, safety advocates, insurance companies, and concerned dog owners need to keep pressing for the development of a standard for dog safety equipment, to insist that all such equipment pass a government regulated crash test before being sold as safe for travel.

By far, the safest travel arrangement for any dog is to secure them inside a kennel, followed by finding a safety restraint that is crash and strength tested and certified to be safe for your dog.

**b) Kennels**

If you opt to contain your best friend inside a kennel, crate or travel bag, you absolutely must make sure that the kennel or bag is very securely attached with the vehicle's seatbelt system or even better, with special tie downs that are bolted to the floor of the vehicle.

A dog kennel or crate will easily fit on the back seat of most vehicles, especially one small enough to fit a Teacup Yorkie, and can be secured with the vehicle's restraint system. A Teacup Yorkie riding inside a kennel inside your vehicle will have the best protection in the case of a rollover accident.

**c) Harness Restraints**

The Kurgo Tru-Fit Smart harness has been crash and strength tested and with its steel nesting buckles has a tensile strength tested to withstand a force of 2250 pounds (1020 kilogram-force). The crash test videos of this product depict a 35-pound (15.9

kilogram) dummy dog traveling at 30 miles per hour (48.28 km/h), recorded at an accredited University test facility.

The Ruff Rider Roadie® harness successfully passed the preliminary test criteria for both dynamic and static load limits. Ruff Rider's only product is the Roadie® travel restraint which was invented by dog owner, Carl Goldberg, after his pet was ejected through the front windshield of his vehicle during a minor collision.

The design of the Roadie® is so unique that it was awarded three (3) patents, and over the past 20 years Roadie® has helped protect many dogs during vehicle accidents.

Sleepypod™ manufactures a safety harness called *"Clickit Utility"* that has a #1 safety rating. Apparently, this harness is the first dog safety harness to incorporate three-points of attachment to better absorb force caused in a front end collision by effectively dissipating energy while keeping the dog in the car seat during an impact (patents pending).

The Clickit Utility harness can also be used in the cargo area and includes a d-ring on the back of the vest so it can be used as a walking harness.

Keep your Teacup Yorkie safe when traveling in your vehicle. Do your research and either transport your dog inside a kennel, or find a safety harness that is both strength tested and certified to be able to keep your Teacup Yorkie safe in the event of an accident.

### d) Sherpa for Small Dogs

*"Sherpa"* is a name that refers to a soft-sided dog carrier with zippered pockets for carrying important papers, treats, bags, etc., that has mesh sides for superior ventilation.

*Chapter 10: Daily Feeding and Care*

---

While there is an actual "Sherpa" brand name, this name has become synonymous with any type of soft-sided carrier bag.

The Sherpa bag has handles as well as a shoulder strap and some even have wheels, so your smaller Teacup Yorkie puppy will be able to safely travel anywhere in style and comfort.

A Teacup Yorkie will be the perfect candidate for learning to travel about inside a Sherpa or soft-sided travel bag, such as the Sleepypod™.

When they are young puppies, get them used to Sherpa travel by putting them inside their bag every time they need to go outside, and before you bring them back inside. When you do this, a Teacup Yorkie puppy will very quickly learn to love scooting into their bag because they associate it with the fun activity of going outside with you.

Once your Teacup Yorkie puppy becomes used to Sherpa travel, it will be very easy for them to travel with you wherever you go, including public transportation (buses), boats, planes and vehicles, and the best way to start them getting used to this idea is as soon as you bring your new puppy home.

Every time you go to your vehicle, put your Teacup Yorkie inside their Sherpa bag and pretty soon they will associate fun adventures with the Sherpa and will not hesitate to quickly hop inside.

*"Sleepypod™"* manufactures various styles of higher end travel bags for smaller dogs, and puts their bags through rigorous crash testing to ensure they are totally safe.

Although these bags are considerably more costly than many other canine travel bags, you will have peace of mind knowing that your Teacup Yorkie will always be safe when riding inside one.

**e) Air Travel**

A tiny Teacup Yorkies will easily be able to travel inside a Sherpa bag inside the airplane cabin as *"carry on baggage"* if the carrier conforms to the airline regulations, which state that a pet carrier must be able to fit under the seat in front of you.

Most soft carriers are airline approved and under seat dimensions are generally as follows:

**Window Seat**: 19" L x 14" W x 8.25" H
[48.26 cm L x 35.56 cm W x 20.955 cm H]
**Middle Seat**: 19" L x 19" W x 8.25" H
[48.26 cm L x 48.26 cm W x 20.955 cm H]
**Aisle Seat**: 19" L x 14" W x 8.25" H
[48.26 cm L x 35.56 cm W x 20.955 cm H]

For in-cabin travel by plane, your dog must be able to stand up and turn around comfortably inside the bag. Airlines also require an absorbent liner in the bag, which could be a pee pad, an old towel, a favorite blanket, or a cozy, faux lambskin liner.

Many styles of canine carrier bags are officially approved for airline travel, and when you make your flight reservations, don't forget to reserve for your Teacup Yorkie as well because there is generally a small charge for in-cabin travel and some airlines will only permit a certain number of canine travelers per flight.

# Chapter 11: House Training

## 1. Human Training

House training, house breaking, or *"potty"* training, is a critical first step in the education of any new puppy, and the first part of a successful process is training the human guardian.

When you bring home your new Teacup Yorkie puppy, they will be relying upon your guidance to teach them what they need to learn.

When you provide your puppy with your consistent patience and understanding, they are capable of learning rules at a very early age, and house training is no different, especially since it's all about establishing a regular routine.

Potty training a new puppy takes time and patience — how much time depends entirely upon you.

Check in with yourself and make sure your energy remains consistently calm and patient and that you exercise plenty of compassion and understanding while you help your new puppy learn their new bathroom rules.

Teacup Yorkie puppies and dogs flourish with routines and happily, so do humans, therefore, the first step is to establish a daily routine that will work well for both canine and human alike.

For instance, depending upon the age of your Teacup Yorkie puppy, make a plan to take them out for a bathroom break every two hours and stick to it because while you are in the beginning stages of potty training, the more vigilant and consistent you can be, the quicker and more successful your results will be.

## Chapter 11: House Training

Generally speaking, while your puppy is still growing, a young puppy can hold it approximately one hour for every month of their age.

This means that if your 2-month-old puppy has been happily snoozing for a couple of hours, as soon as they wake up, they will need to go outside.

Some of the first indications or signs that your puppy needs to be taken outside to relieve themselves will be when you see them:

- Sniffing around
- Circling
- Looking for or approaching the door
- Whining, crying or barking
- Acting agitated

It will be important to always take your Teacup Yorkie puppy out first thing every morning, and immediately after they wake up from a nap as well as soon after they have finished eating a meal or having a big drink of water.

Also, your happy praise goes a long way toward encouraging and reinforcing future success when your Teacup Yorkie puppy makes the right decisions, so let them know you are happy when they do their business in the right place.

Initially, treats can be a good way to reinforce how pleased you are that your puppy is learning to go potty in the right place. Slowly treats can be removed and replaced with your happy praise.

Next, now that you have a new puppy in your life, you will want to be flexible with respect to adapting your schedule to meet the requirements that will help to quickly teach your Teacup Yorkie puppy their new bathroom routine.

## Chapter 11: House Training

This means not leaving your puppy alone for endless hours at a time because firstly, they are sensitive pack animals that need companionship and your direction at all times, plus long periods alone will result in the disruption of the potty training schedule you have worked hard to establish.

If you have no choice but to leave your puppy alone for many hours, make sure that you place them in a paper lined room or pen where they can relieve themselves without destroying your favorite carpet or new hardwood flooring.

Remember, your Teacup Yorkie is a growing puppy with a bladder and bowels that they do not yet have complete control over and you will have a much happier time and better success if you simply train yourself to pay attention to when your young companion is showing signs of needing to relieve themselves.

## 2. Bell Training

A very easy way to introduce your new Teacup Yorkie puppy to house training is to begin by teaching them how to ring a doorbell whenever they need to go outside.

Ringing a doorbell is not only a convenient alert system for both you and your Teacup Yorkie puppy or dog, your visitors will be most impressed by how smart your Teacup Yorkie is.

A further benefit of training your puppy to ring a bell is that you will not have to listen to your puppy or dog whining, barking or howling to be let out, and your door will not become scratched up from their nails.

Unless you prefer to purchase an already manufactured doggy doorbell or system, take a trip to your local novelty store and purchase a small bell that has a nice, loud ring.

Attach the bell to a piece of ribbon or string and hang it from a door handle or tape it to a door sill near the door where you will be taking your puppy out when they need to relieve themselves. The string will need to be long enough so that your Teacup Yorkie puppy can easily reach the bell with their nose or a paw.

Next, each time you take your puppy out to go potty, say the word *"Out"*, and use their paw or their nose to ring the bell. Praise them for this *"trick"* and immediately take them outside.

The only down side to teaching your Teacup Yorkie puppy or dog to ring a bell when they want to go outside, is that even if they don't actually have to go out to relieve themselves, but just want to go outside because they are bored, you will still have to take them out every time they ring the bell.

There are many types and styles of *"gotta' go"* commercially manufactured bells you could choose, ranging from the elegant **"Poochie Bells™"** that hang from a doorknob, the simple **"Tell Bell™"** that sits on the floor, or various high tech door chime systems that function much like a doggy intercom system where they push a pad with their paw and it rings a bell.

Whatever doorbell system you choose for your Teacup Yorkie puppy, once they are trained, this type of an alert system is a simple and easy way to eliminate accidents in the home.

## 3. Kennel Training

Kennel training is always a good idea for any puppy early in their education, because it can be utilized for many different situations, including keeping them safe while traveling inside a vehicle and being a very helpful tool for house training.

When purchasing a kennel for your Teacup Yorkie puppy, always buy a kennel that will be the correct size for your puppy once they become an adult.

The kennel will be the correct size if an adult Teacup Yorkie can stand up and easily turn around inside their kennel.

When you train your Teacup Yorkie puppy to accept sleeping in their own kennel at nighttime, this will also help to accelerate their potty training, because no puppy or dog wants to relieve themselves where they sleep, which means that they will hold their bladder and bowels as long as they possibly can.

Always be kind and compassionate and remember that a puppy will be able to hold it approximately one hour for every month of their age.

Generally, a Teacup Yorkie puppy that is three months old will be able to hold it for approximately three hours, unless they just ate a meal or had a big drink of water.

Be watchful and consistent so that you learn your Teacup Yorkie puppy's body language, which will alert you to when it's time for them to go outside.

Presenting them with familiar scents, by taking them to the same spot in the yard or the same street corner, bush or tree, will help to remind and encourage them that they are outside to relieve themselves.

Use a voice cue to remind your puppy why they are outside, such as *"go pee"* and always remember to praise them every time they relieve themselves in the right place so that they quickly understand what you expect of them and will learn to *"go"* on cue.

## 4. Exercise Pen Training

The exercise pen is a transition from kennel only training and will be helpful for those times when you may have to leave your Teacup Yorkie puppy for more hours than they can reasonably be expected to hold it.

## Chapter 11: House Training

During those times when you must be away from the home for several hours, it's time to introduce your Teacup Yorkie puppy to an exercise pen.

Exercise pens are usually constructed of wire sections that you can put together in whatever shape you desire, and the pen needs to be large enough to hold your puppy's kennel inside one half of the pen, while the other half will be lined with newspapers or pee pads.

Place your Teacup Yorkie puppy's food and water dishes next to the kennel and leave the kennel door open, so they can wander in and out whenever they wish, to eat or drink or go to the papers or pads if they need to relieve themselves.

Your puppy will be contained in a small area of your home while you are away and because they are already used to sleeping inside their kennel, they will not want to relieve themselves inside the area where they sleep. Therefore, your Teacup Yorkie puppy will naturally go to the other half of the pen to relieve themselves on the newspapers or pee pads.

This method will help train your puppy to be quickly "paper" trained when you must leave them alone for a few hours.

## 5. Puppy Apartment™ Training

A similar and more costly alternative, the *Puppy Apartment*™ is a step up from the exercise pen training system that makes the process of crate or pen training even easier on both humans and puppies.

The Puppy Apartment™ works well in a variety of situations, whether you're at home and unable to pay close attention to your Teacup Yorkie puppy's needs, whether you must be away from the home for a few hours or during the evening when everyone is asleep and you don't particularly want to get up at 3:00 a.m. to take your Teacup Yorkie puppy out to go pee.

## Chapter 11: House Training

The Puppy Apartment™ is an innovation that is convenient for both puppy and human alike.

What makes this system so effective is the patent pending dividing wall with a door leading to the other side, all inside the pen.

One side of the Puppy Apartment™ is where the puppy's bed is located and the other side (through the doorway) is the bathroom area that is lined with pee pads.

With the bathroom right next door, your Teacup Yorkie puppy or dog can take a bathroom break whenever they wish, without the need to alert family members to let them out.

This one bedroom, one bathroom system, which is a combination of the kennel/training pen, is a great alternative for helping to eliminate the stress of worrying about always keeping a watchful eye on your puppy or getting up during the night to take them outside every few hours to help them avoid making mistakes.

According to Modern Puppies...

> *"The Puppy Apartment™ takes the MESSY out of paper training, the ODORS AND HASSLES out of artificial grass training, MISSING THE MARK out of potty pad training and HAVING TO HOLD IT out of crate training. House training a puppy has never been faster or easier!*
>
> *The Puppy Apartment™ has taken all the benefits of the most popular potty training methods and combined them into one magical device and potty training system. This device and system has revolutionized how modern puppies are potty trained!"*

## Chapter 11: House Training

Manufactured in the United States, this product ships directly from the California supplier (Modern Puppies).

Pricing of the Puppy Apartment™ begins at $138. USD (£83.37) and is only available online at Modern Puppies.

## 6. Free Training

If you would rather not confine your young Teacup Yorkie puppy to one or two rooms in your home, and will be allowing them to freely range about your home anywhere they wish during the day, this is considered free training.

When free house training your Teacup Yorkie puppy, you will need to closely watch your puppy's activities all day long so that you can be aware of the *"signs"* that will indicate when they need to go outside to relieve themselves.

For instance, circling and sniffing is a sure sign that they are looking for a place to do their business.

Never get upset or scold a puppy for having an accident inside the home, because this will result in teaching your puppy to be afraid of you and to only relieve themselves in secret places or when you're not watching.

If you catch your Teacup Yorkie puppy making a mistake, all that is necessary is for you to calmly say *"No"*, and quickly scoop them up and take them outside or to their indoor bathroom area.

From your sensitive puppy's point of view, yelling or screaming when they make a potty mistake, will be understood by your puppy or dog as unstable energy being displayed by the person who is supposed to be their leader. This type of unstable behavior will only teach your puppy to fear and disrespect you.

When you are vigilant, the Teacup Yorkie should not a difficult puppy to housebreak and they will generally do very well when you start them off with *"puppy pee pads"* that you will move

## Chapter 11: House Training

closer and closer to the same door that you always use when taking them outside. This way they will quickly learn to associate going to this door when they need to relieve themselves.

When you pay close attention to your Teacup Yorkie puppy's sleeping, eating, drinking and playing habits, you will quickly learn their body language so that you are able to predict when they might need to relieve themselves.

Your Teacup Yorkie puppy will always need to relieve themselves first thing in the morning, as soon as they wake up from a nap, approximately 20 minutes after they finish eating a meal, after they have finished a play session, and of course, before they go to bed at night.

It's important to have compassion during this house training time in your young Teacup Yorkie's life so that their education will be as stress-free as possible.

It's also important to be vigilant because how well you pay attention will minimize the opportunities your puppy may have for making a bathroom mistake in the first place, and the fewer mistakes they make, the sooner your Teacup Yorkie puppy will be house trained.

## 7. Mistakes Happen

Remember that a dog's sense of smell is at least 2,000 times more sensitive that our human sense of smell.

As a result of your Teacup Yorkie puppy's superior sense of smell, it will be very important to effectively remove all odors from house training accidents, because otherwise, your Teacup Yorkie puppy will be attracted by the smell to the place where they may have had a previous accident, and will want to do their business there again and again.

While there are many products that are supposed to remove odors and stains, many of these are not very effective. You want a professional grade cleaner that will not just mask one odor with another scent, you want a product that will completely neutralize odors.

**TIP**: go to RemoveUrineOdors.com and order yourself some *"SUN"* and/or *"Max Enzyme"* because these products contain professional-strength odor neutralizers and urine digesters that bind to and completely absorb odors on any type of surface.

## 8. Electronic Training Devices

Generally speaking, positive training methods are far more effective than using devices that involve negative stimulation.

Further, unless you are training a Teacup Yorkie to hunt rats or mice, using electronic devices is usually a excuse for a lazy human who will not take the time to properly train their dog by teaching them rules and boundaries which leads to respect and an attentive follower.

When you do not provide your Teacup Yorkie (or any dog) with a consistent leadership role that teaches your dog to trust, respect and listen to you in all circumstances, you will inevitably experience behavioral issues.

Electronic training devices such as e-collars, spray collars or electronic fencing all rely upon negative, painful or stressful reinforcement, which can easily cause a sensitive breed, like the Teacup Yorkie, to become nervous or live a neurotic life of fear.

For instance, a dog simply cannot understand the principles of "invisible" boundaries, and therefore, should never be subjected to the confusion of the punishment that occurs when walking across an invisible line within their own home territory.

Dogs naturally understand the positive training methods of receiving a reward, which is not only much more efficient and effective when teaching boundaries, rewards are far kinder, and create a much stronger bond with your dog.

## a) The Truth About Shock Collars

First of all, it would have to be an extremely rare situation in which it would be necessary or recommended that you use a shock collar on a tiny Teacup Yorkie as these devices are usually only employed in extreme situations, and generally for much larger breeds who could seriously harm someone.

The use of remote, electronic, shock or *"e-collars"* is at best a controversial subject that can quickly escalate into heated arguments.

In certain, rare circumstances, and when used correctly, the e-collar can be a helpful training tool that could actually save a dog's life if they are acting out in dangerous ways that could seriously harm or even kill them.

An e-collar would generally be utilized in a circumstance where a larger breed of dog has access to free range over a large property, resulting in difficulties getting their attention from a distance if they become distracted by other animals or smells.

Many dogs that have not been properly trained from a young age also learn that when they are off leash and out of your immediate reach that they can choose to ignore your commands, bark their heads off, terrorize the neighbors or chase wildlife.

All of these situations are generally not activities that a Teacup Yorkie would have the slightest interest in, unless they have access to a large property and their hunting instinct kicks in, because they would prefer being at home with their humans.

Generally e-collars can be effective training tools for working breed herding, hunting or tracking dogs.

In these types of circumstances a remote training collar can be an effective training device for reinforcing verbal commands from a great distance, such as "Come", "Sit" or "Stay".

Finally, electronic collars can be used as a last resort to help teach a dog not to engage in a dangerous behavior that could result in them being seriously harmed or even killed.

**b) Electronic Fencing**

Honestly, there are far more reasons NOT to install an electronic fence as a means of keeping your dog inside your yard, than there are good reasons for considering one.

In most cases, humans who install electronic fencing because they are worried that their dog will run away have simply not taken the time to develop a relationship of trust and respect with their canine companion.

For instance, a dog whose yard is surrounded by an electronic fence can quite easily develop fear, aggression, or both, directed toward what they may believe is the cause of the shock they are receiving.

As a result, installing an electronic fence may actually teach your Teacup Yorkie to become aggressive toward cats, other dogs, other humans, other wildlife, children riding by on bikes or skateboards, the mail carrier, or the people next door.

As well, a dog that receives a fright, or in excitement forgets about the shock they are going to receive, may run through an electronic fence and then be too frightened or stressed to come back home because it means that they must pass through the painful barrier again.

Further, it is actually possible that electronic fencing may encourage a dog to escape the yard simply because they associate their yard with pain. This feeling can be reinforced if a dog

## Chapter 11: House Training

escapes the electronic yard and then is again punished by the shock when they attempt to come home.

Another factor to keep in mind with respect to electronic fencing is that other dogs or teasing children can freely enter the yard and torment or attack your dog, and a thief bent on stealing your Teacup Yorkie will be able to do so with ease.

In the case of a very small Teacup Yorkie, allowing them to be alone in the yard also puts them in danger of being snatched up by a large predator bird that can easily swoop in from overhead.

The absolute best way to keep your dog safe in their own yard, while helping to establish your role as guardian and leader, is to be out there with them while they are on leash, and to only permit them freedom in your yard under your close supervision.

# Chapter 12: Medical Care & Safety

## 1. Choosing a Veterinarian

A consideration to keep in mind when choosing a veterinarian clinic will be that some clinics specialize in caring for smaller pets, and some specialize in larger animal care, while still others have a wide ranging area of expertise and will care for all animals, including livestock and reptiles.

Choosing a clinic will be a personal decision, however, since the Teacup Yorkie is considered a smaller breed of dog, your dog's needs may be better served by choosing a clinic that specializes in the care of smaller pets.

Choosing a good veterinary clinic will be very similar to choosing the right health care clinic or doctor for your own personal health because you want to ensure that your Teacup Yorkie puppy receives the quality care they deserve.

Begin your search by asking other dog owners where they take their fur friends and whether they are happy with the service they receive.

If you don't know anyone to ask, visit the local pet store in your area as they should be able to provide you with references and local listings of pet care clinics.

Next, check online, because a good pet clinic will have an active website up and running that will list details of all the services they provide along with an overview of all staff members, their education and qualifications.

Once you've narrowed your search, it's time to personally visit the clinics you may be interested in, as this will be a good opportunity for you to visually inspect the facility, interact with the staff and perhaps meet the veterinarians face to face.

Of course, it's not just you who needs to feel comfortable with the clinic chosen and those working there. Your puppy needs to feel comfortable, too, and this is where visiting a clinic and interacting with the staff and veterinarians will provide you with an idea of their experience and expertise in handling your puppy.

If your puppy is comfortable with them, then you will be much more likely to trust that they will be providing the best care for your puppy who will need to receive all their vaccinations and yearly check-ups, and eventually be spayed or neutered.

It's also a good idea to take your puppy into your chosen clinic several times before they actually need to be there for any treatment, so that they are not fearful of the new smells and unfamiliar surroundings.

## 2. Neutering and Spaying

While it can sometimes be difficult to find the definitive answer when asking when is the best time to neuter or spay your young Teacup Yorkie, because there are varying opinions on this topic, one thing that most veterinarians do agree on is that earlier spaying or neutering, between 4 and 6 months of age, is a better choice than waiting.

Spaying or neutering surgeries are carried out under general anesthesia, and as more dogs are being neutered at younger ages, speak with your veterinarian and ask for their recommendations regarding the right age to spay or neuter your Teacup Yorkie.

### a) Effects on Aggression

Intact (non-neutered) males and females are more likely to display aggression related to sexual behavior than are dogs that have been neutered or spayed.

Fighting, particularly in male dogs that is directed at other males, is less common after neutering, and the intensity of other types of aggression, such as irritable aggression in females will be totally eliminated by spaying.

While neutering or spaying is not a treatment for aggression, it can certainly help to minimize the severity and escalation of aggressiveness and is often the first step toward resolving an aggressive behavior problem.

**b) What is Neutering?**

Neutering is a surgical procedure, carried out by a licensed veterinarian surgeon to render a male dog unable to reproduce.

In males, the surgery is also referred to as *"castration"* because the procedure entails the removal of the young dog's testicles. When the testicles are removed, what is left behind is an empty scrotal sac (which used to contain the puppy's testicles) and this empty sac will soon shrink in size until it is no longer noticeable.

**c) Neutering Males**

Neutering male Teacup Yorkie puppies before they are six months of age can help to ensure that they will be less likely to suffer from obesity problems when they grow older.

Neutering can also mean that a male Teacup Yorkie will be less likely to have the urge to wander.

Further, waiting until a male Teacup Yorkie is older than six months before having them neutered could mean that they will experience the effects of raging testosterone that will drive them to escape their yards by any means necessary to search out females to mate with.

Non-neutered males also tend to spray or mark territory much more often, both inside and outside the home, and during this time can start to display aggressive tendencies toward other dogs as well as people.

**d) What is Spaying?**

In female puppies, sterilization, referred to as *"spaying"* is a surgical procedure carried out by a licensed veterinarian, to prevent the female dog from becoming pregnant and to stop regular heat cycles.

The sterilization procedure is much more involved for a female puppy (than for a male), as it requires the removal of both ovaries and the uterus by incision into the puppy's abdominal cavity. The uterus is also removed during this surgery, to prevent the possibility of it becoming infected later on in life.

**e) Spaying Females**

Preferably, female Teacup Yorkie puppies should be spayed before their very first estrus or heat cycle. Females in heat often appear more agitated and irritable, while sleeping and eating less and some may become extremely aggressive toward other dogs.

Spaying female puppies before their first heat pattern can eliminate these hormonal stressors and reduce the opportunity of mammary glandular tumors. Early spaying also protects against various other potential concerns, such as uterine infections.

**f) Effects on General Temperament**

Many dog owners often become needlessly worried that a neutered or spayed dog will lose their vigor.
Rest assured that a dog's personality or energy level will not be modified or altered in any way by the neutering process, and in fact, many unfavorable qualities resulting from hormonal impact may resolve after surgery.

## Chapter 12: Medical Care & Safety

Your Teacup Yorkie will certainly not come to be less caring or cheerful, and neither will he or she resent you because you are not denying your dog any essential encounters. You will, however, be acting as a conscientious, informed, and caring Teacup Yorkie guardian.

Further, there is little evidence to suggest that the nature of a female Teacup Yorkie will improve after having a litter of puppies.

What is important is that you do not project your own psychological needs or concerns onto your Teacup Yorkie puppy, because there is no gain to be had from permitting sexual activity in either male or female canines.

For instance, it is not *"abnormal"* or *"mean"* to manage a puppy's reproductive activity by having them sterilized. Rather, it is unkind and irresponsible not to neuter or spay a dog and there are many positive benefits of having this procedure carried out.

**g) Effects on Escape and Roaming**

A neutered or spayed Teacup Yorkie is less likely to wander. Castrated male dogs have the tendency to patrol smaller sized outdoor areas and are less likely to participate in territorial conflicts with perceived opponents.

**NOTE**: a Teacup Yorkie that has actually already experienced successful escapes from the yard may continue to wander after they are spayed or neutered.

**h) Effects on Problem Elimination**

An unsterilized dog may urinate or defecate inside the home or in other undesirable areas in an attempt to stake territorial claims, relieve anxiety, or advertise their available reproductive status.

## Chapter 12: Medical Care & Safety

While neutering or spaying a Teacup Yorkie puppy after they have already begun to inappropriately eliminate or mark territory to announce their sexual availability to other dogs will reduce the more powerful urine odor as well as eliminate the hormonal factors, once this habit has begun, the undesirable behavior may continue to persist after neutering or spaying.

**i) Possible Weight Gain**

While metabolic changes that occur after spaying or neutering can cause some Teacup Yorkie puppy's to gain weight, often the real culprit for any weight gain is the human who feels guilty for subjecting their puppy to any kind of pain and therefore, they attempt to make themselves feel better by feeding more treats or meals to their Teacup Yorkie companion.

If you are concerned about weight gain after neutering or spaying a Teacup Yorkie puppy, simply adjust their food and treat consumption, as needed, and make sure that they receive adequate daily exercise.

It's a very simply process to change your Teacup Yorkie's food intake according to their physical demands and how they look, and if your Teacup Yorkie puppy's daily exercise and level of activity has not changed after they have been spayed or neutered, there will likely be no change in food management necessary.

## 3. Why Vaccinate a Puppy?

Puppies need to be vaccinated by a veterinarian in order to provide them with protection against four common and serious diseases.
Vaccination against this common set of diseases is referred to as *"DAPP"*, which stands for **D**istemper, **A**denovirus, **P**arainfluenza and **P**arvo Virus.

Approximate one week after your Teacup Yorkie puppy has completed all three sets of primary DAPP vaccinations they will be fully protected from those specific diseases. Thereafter, most veterinarians will recommend a once a year vaccination for the next year or two.

It has now become common practice to vaccinate adult dogs every three years, and if your veterinarian is insisting on a yearly vaccination for your Teacup Yorkie puppy, you need to ask them why, because to do otherwise is considered by most professionals to be *"over vaccinating"*.

## a) Distemper

Canine distemper is a contagious and serious viral illness for which there is currently no known cure.

This deadly virus, which is spread either through the air or by direct or indirect contact with a dog that is already infected, or other distemper carrying wildlife, including ferrets, raccoons, foxes, skunks and wolves, is a relative of the measles virus which affects humans.

Canine distemper is sometimes also called *"hard pad disease"* because some strains of the distemper virus actually cause thickening of the pads on a dog's feet, which can also affect the end of a dog's nose.

In dogs or animals with weak immune systems, death may result two to five weeks after the initial distemper infection.

Early symptoms of distemper include fever, loss of appetite, and mild eye inflammation that may only last a day or two. Symptoms become more serious and noticeable as the disease progresses. A puppy or dog that survives the distemper virus will usually continue to experience symptoms or signs of the disease throughout their remaining lifespan, including *"hard pad disease"* as well as *"enamel hypoplasia"*, which is damage to the enamel of the puppy's teeth that are not yet formed or that have not yet pushed through the gums.

Enamel hypoplasia is caused when the distemper virus kills the cells that manufacture tooth enamel.

**b) Adenovirus**

Is a virus that causes infectious canine hepatitis, which can range in severity from very mild to very serious, sometimes resulting in death.

Symptoms can include coughing, loss of appetite, increased thirst and urination, tiredness, runny eyes and nose, vomiting, bruising or bleeding under the skin, swelling of the head, neck and body, fluid accumulation in the abdomen area, jaundice (yellow tinge to the skin), a bluish clouding of the cornea of the eye (called "hepatitis blue eye") and seizures.

There is no specific treatment for infectious canine hepatitis. Treatment of the disease is focused on managing symptoms while the virus runs its course. Hospitalization and intravenous fluid therapy may be required in severe cases.

**c) Canine Parainfluenza Virus**

The canine parainfluenza virus (CPIV) also referred to as *"canine influenza virus"*, *"greyhound disease"* or *"race flu"*, which is easily spread through the air or by coming into contact with respiratory secretions, was originally a virus that only affected horses.

This disease is believed to have adapted to become contagious to dogs, is easily spread from dog to dog, and may cause symptoms that become fatal.

While the more frequent occurrences of this respiratory infection are seen in areas where there are high dog populations, such as race tracks, boarding kennels and pet stores, this virus is highly contagious to any dog or puppy, at any age.

## Chapter 12: Medical Care & Safety

Symptoms can include a dry, hacking cough, difficulty breathing, wheezing, runny nose and eyes, sneezing, fever, loss of appetite, tiredness, depression and possible pneumonia.

In cases where only a cough exists, tests will be required to determine whether the cause of the cough is the parainfluenza virus or the less serious *"kennel cough"*.

While many dogs can naturally recover from this virus, they will remain contagious, and for this reason, in order to prevent the spread to other animals, aggressive treatment of the virus, with antibiotics and antiviral drugs will be the general course of action.

In more severe cases, a cough suppressant may be prescribed, as well as intravenous fluids to help prevent secondary bacterial infection.

### d) Canine Parvovirus

Canine parvovirus (CPV) is a highly contagious viral illness affecting puppies and dogs. Parvovirus also affects other canine species including foxes, coyotes and wolves.

There are two forms of this virus (1) the more common intestinal form, and (2) the less common cardiac form, which can cause death in young puppies.

Symptoms of the intestinal form of parvovirus include vomiting, bloody diarrhea, weight loss, and lack of appetite, while the less common cardiac form attacks the heart muscle.

Early vaccination in young puppies has radically reduced the incidence of canine parvovirus infection, which is easily transmitted either by direct contact with an infected dog, or indirectly, by sniffing an infected dog's feces.

The virus can also be brought into a dog's environment on the bottom of human shoes that may have stepped on infected feces, and there is evidence that this hardy virus can live in ground soil for up to a year.

Recovery from parvovirus requires both aggressive and early treatment. With proper treatment, death rates are relatively low (between 5 and 20%), although chances of survival for puppies are much lower than for older dogs, and in all instances, there is no guarantee of survival.

Treatment of parvovirus requires hospitalization where intravenous fluids and nutrients are administered to help combat dehydration. As well, antibiotics will be given to counteract secondary bacterial infections, and as necessary, medications to control nausea and vomiting may also be given.

Without prompt and proper treatment, dogs that have severe parvovirus infections can die within 48 to 72 hours.

## 4. Other Diseases and Viruses

### a) Rabies Vaccinations

Rabies is a viral disease transmitted by coming into contact with the saliva of an infected animal, usually through a bite.

The virus travels to the brain along the nerves and once symptoms develop, death is almost certainly inevitable, usually following a prolonged period of suffering.

If you plan to travel out of State or across country borders, you will need to make sure that your Teacup Yorkie has an up to date Rabies Vaccination Certificate (NASPHV form 51) indicating they have been inoculated against rabies.

Vaccinating dogs against rabies is also compulsory in most countries in mainland Europe, as is permanent identification and registration of dogs through the use of a Pet Passport.

Those living in a country that is rabies free (UK, Eire) are not required to vaccinate their dogs against rabies, unless they intend to travel.

**b) Leishmaniasis**

Leishmaniasis is caused by a parasite and is transmitted by a bite from a sand fly.

There is no definitive answer for effectively combating Leishmaniasis, especially since one vaccine will not prevent the known multiple species.

In areas where the known cause is a sand fly, deltamethrin collars (containing a neurotoxic insecticide) worn by the dogs has been proven to be 86% effective.

There are two types of Leishmaniasis: (1) a skin reaction causing hair loss, lesions and ulcerative dermatitis, and (2) a more severe, abdominal organ reaction, which is also known as *"black fever"*. When the disease affects organs of the abdominal cavity the symptoms include:

- Loss of appetite
- Diarrhea
- Severe weight loss
- Exercise intolerance
- Vomiting
- Nose bleed
- Tarry feces
- Fever
- Pain in the joints
- Excessive thirst and urination
- Inflammation of the muscles

Leishmaniasis spreads throughout the body to most organs, with kidney failure being the most common cause of death. Virtually all infected dogs develop this system wide disease and as much as 90% of those infected will also display skin reactions.

Affected dogs in the US are frequently found to have acquired this infection in another country.

Of note, is that this disease is regularly found in the Middle East, the area around the Mediterranean basin, Portugal, Spain, Africa, South and Central America, southern Mexico and the US, with regular cases reported in Oklahoma and Ohio, where it is found in 20 to 40% of the dog population.

There have also been a few reported cases in Switzerland, northern France and the Netherlands.

**NOTE:** Leishmaniasis is a *"zoonotic"* infection, which is a contagious disease that can be spread between both animals and humans.

This means that the organisms residing in the Leishmaniasis lesions can be communicated to humans.

Treatment in dogs is often difficult and the dog may suffer from relapses. Leishmaniasis poses a significant risk to the health of your dog, especially if you travel to the Mediterranean.

**c) Lyme Disease**

This is one of the most common tick-borne diseases in the world, which is transmitted by Borrelia bacteria found in the deer or sheep tick.

Lyme disease, also called *"borreliosis"*, is also a zoonotic disease that can affect both humans and dogs and this disease can be fatal.

The Borrelia bacteria that causes Lyme's disease, is transmitted by slow-feeding, hard-shelled deer or sheep ticks, and the tick usually has to be attached to the dog for a minimum of 18 hours before the infection is transmitted.

Symptoms of this disease in a young or adult dog include:

- Recurrent lameness from joint inflammation
- Loss of appetite
- Depression
- Stiff walk with arched back
- Sensitivity to touch
- Swollen lymph nodes
- Fever
- Kidney damage
- Rare heart or nervous system complications

While Lyme disease has been reported in dogs throughout the United States and Europe, it is most prevalent in the upper Mid-Western states, the Atlantic seaboard, and the Pacific coastal states.

In order to properly diagnose and treat Lyme disease, blood tests will be required, and if the tests are positive, oral antibiotics will be prescribed to treat the conditions.

Prevention is the key to keeping this disease under control because dogs that have had Lyme disease before are still able to get the disease again.

There is a vaccine for Lyme disease and dogs living in areas that have easy access to these ticks should be vaccinated yearly.

**d) Rocky Mountain Spotted Fever**

This tick-transmitted disease is very often seen in dogs in the East, Midwest, and plains region of the US, and the organisms causing Rocky Mountain Spotted Fever (RMSF) are transmitted by both the American dog tick and the RMSF tick, which must be attached to the dog for a minimum of five hours in order to transmit the disease.

Common symptoms of RMSF include:

- Fever
- Reduced appetite
- Depression
- Pain in the joints
- Lameness
- Vomiting
- Diarrhea

Some dogs affected with RMSF may develop heart abnormalities, pneumonia, kidney failure, liver damage, or even neurological signs, such an seizures or unsteady, wobbly or stumbling gait.

Diagnosis of this disease requires blood testing and if the results are positive, oral antibiotics will be given to the infected dog for approximately two weeks.

Dogs that can clear the organism from their systems will recover and after being infected, will remain immune to future infection.

**e) Ehrlichiosis**

This is another tick borne disease transmitted by both the brown dog tick and the Lone Star Tick.

Ehrlichiosis has been reported in every state in the US, as well as worldwide. Common symptoms include:

- Depression
- Reduced appetite
- Fever
- Stiff and painful joints
- Bruising

Signs of infection typically occur less than a month after a tick bite and last for approximately four weeks. There is no vaccine available.

Blood tests may be required to test for antibodies and treatment will require a course of antibiotics for up to four weeks in order to completely clear the organism from the infected dog's system.

After a dog has been previously infected, they may develop antibodies to the organism, but will not be immune to being re-infected.

Dogs living in areas of the country where the Ehrlichiosis tick disease are common or widespread may be prescribed low doses of antibiotics during tick season.

**f) Anaplasmosis**

Deer ticks and Western blacklegged ticks are carriers of the bacteria that transmit canine Anaplasmosis.

However, there is also another form of Anaplasmosis (caused by a different bacteria) that is carried by the brown dog tick. Because the deer tick also carries other diseases, some animals may be at risk for developing more than one tick-borne disease at the same time.

Signs of Anaplasmosis are similar to Ehrlichiosis and include painful joints, diarrhea, fever, and vomiting as well as possible nervous system disorders.

A dog will usually begin to show signs of Anaplasmosis within a couple of weeks after infection and diagnosis will require blood and urine testing, and sometimes other specialized laboratory tests.

Treatment is with oral antibiotics for up to 30 days, depending on how severe the infection may be.

## Chapter 12: Medical Care & Safety

When this disease is quickly treated, most dogs will recover completely, however, subsequent immunity is not guaranteed, which means that a dog may be re-infected if exposed again.

**g) Tick Paralysis**

Tick paralysis is caused when ticks secrete a toxin that affects the nervous system.

Affected dogs show signs of weakness and limpness approximately one week after being first bitten by ticks.

Symptoms usual begin with a change in pitch of the dog's usual bark, which will become softer, and weakness in the rear legs that eventually involves all four legs, which is then followed by the dog showing difficulty breathing and swallowing.

If the condition is not diagnosed and properly treated, death can occur.

Treatment involves locating and removing the tick and then treating the infected dog with tick anti-serum.

**h) Canine Coronavirus**

While this highly contagious intestinal disease, which is spread through the feces of contaminated dogs, was first discovered in Germany during 1971 when there was an outbreak in sentry dogs, it is now found worldwide.

This virus can be destroyed by most commonly available disinfectants.

Symptoms include:

- Diarrhea
- Vomiting
- Weight loss or anorexia

While deaths resulting from this disease are rare, and treatment generally requires only medication to relieve the diarrhea, dogs that are more severely affected may require intravenous fluids to combat dehydration.

There is a vaccine available, which is usually given to puppies, because they are more susceptible at a young age. This vaccine is also given to show dogs that have a higher risk of exposure to the disease.

**i) Leptospirosis**

This is a disease that occurs throughout the world that can affect many different kinds of animals, including dogs, and as it is also a zoonotic disease, this means that it can affect humans, too. There is potential for both dogs and humans to die from this disease.

The disease is always present in the environment, which makes it easy for any dog to pick up. This is because it is found in many common animals, such as rats, and wildlife, as well as domestic livestock.

Veterinarians generally see more cases of Leptospirosis in the late summer and fall, which is probably because that is when more pets and wildlife are out and about.

More cases also occur after heavy rain falls.

The disease is most common in mild or tropical climates around the World, and in the US or Canada, it is more common in states or provinces that receive heavy rainfall.

The good news is that you can protect your dog from leptospirosis by vaccination, and while puppies are not routinely vaccinated against leptospirosis because chances of contracting the disease depends upon the lifestyle of the dog as well as the area in which the dog lives, it makes sense to vaccinate against this disease if

## Chapter 12: Medical Care & Safety

you and your dog do live in an area considered a hot spot for leptospirosis, so ask your veterinarian.

City rat populations are a major carrier of leptospirosis.

Cold winter conditions lower the risk because the leptospira organisms do not tolerate the freezing and thawing of near-zero temperatures.

They are killed rapidly by drying, but they persist in standing water, dampness, mud and alkaline conditions.

Most of the infected wild animals and domestic animals that spread leptospirosis do not appear ill.

The leptospira take up residence in the kidneys of infected animals, which can include rats, mice, squirrels, skunks, and raccoons and when these animals void urine, they contaminate their environment with living leptospira.

Dogs usually become infected after sniffing urine or by wading, swimming or drinking contaminated water that has infected urine in it, and this is how the disease passes from animal to animal. As well, the leptospira can also enter through a bite wound or if a dog eats infected material.

## 5. Additional Vaccinations

Depending upon where you and your Teacup Yorkie live, your veterinarian may suggest additional vaccinations to help combat diseases that may be more common in your area.

## 6. When Is a Puppy Vaccinated?

The first vaccination needle is normally given to a puppy around six to eight weeks of age, which means that generally it will be the responsibility of the Teacup Yorkie breeder to ensure that the puppy's first shots have been received before their new owner takes them home.

Thereafter, it will be the new Teacup Yorkie puppy's guardians that will be responsible for ensuring that the next two sets of shots, which are usually given three to four weeks after each other, are given by the new guardian's veterinarian at the proper intervals.

## 7. De-Worming

De-worming kills internal parasites that your dog or puppy may have.

**NOTE**: even though your living conditions may be completely sanitary, it is still possible for your dog to have internal parasites because this has nothing to do with where you live or how clean you keep your dog and your home.

It is recommended by the Center for Disease Control (CDC) that puppies be dewormed every 2 weeks until they are 3 months old, and then every month after that, in order to control worms.

Many veterinarians recommend worming dogs for tapeworm and roundworms every 6-12 months.

## 8. Special Care When Pregnant

As canine pregnancy lasts approximately 63 days, and a Teacup Yorkie female will go into labor within 56 to 66 days after becoming pregnant, a pregnant Teacup Yorkie will require immediate attention when the first signs of pregnancy appear.

Immediately upon noticing signs of pregnancy you will want to take your Teacup Yorkie to your veterinarian to confirm the pregnancy and to receive instructions for the proper feeding and care.

## Chapter 12: Medical Care & Safety

During the first days of pregnancy your Teacup Yorkie may experience morning sickness.

Your veterinarian may recommend increasing food intake or adding an egg or cottage cheese to your Teacup Yorkie's meals and switching to puppy kibble, which is higher in protein, at around the 30 day mark.

As the Teacup Yorkie female becomes heavier with the puppies, she will lose interest in exercising and her other normal activities and will need to sleep more.

When the time for birthing is drawing near, the Teacup Yorkie female will start to display "nesting" characteristics where she will search for a warm and safe place to give birth.

You can help by providing a nesting box and she will likely want to take things into the box to make it more comfortable, such as towels or even a stuffed toy that she will begin to mother.

When the time draws near to whelping, the Teacup Yorkie female may completely lose her appetite and show distress by pacing, panting, and acting uncomfortable.
When the birthing time is near, the dog's temperature needs to be checked, and should be around 100.2 to 100.8 degrees Fahrenheit (37.89 to 38.22 degrees Centigrade).

When her temperature drops to approximately 98 to 99.4 degrees Fahrenheit (36.67 to 37.44 degrees Centigrade), the puppies will usually be born within 24 hours.

If you are at all worried about the birthing process you will want to take the mother Teacup Yorkie immediately to your veterinarian's office.

If all goes well at home, within 5-6 hours of the last puppy's birth, you will need to take the mother and her puppies to your veterinarian for a check up to make sure that she has birthed all puppies and placentas, and that the puppies are all healthy.

## 9. Licensing

Many cities and jurisdictions around the world require that dogs be licensed. Usually a dog license is an identifying tag that the dog will be required to wear on their collar. The tag will have an identifying number and a contact number for the registering organization, so that if someone finds a lost dog wearing a tag, the owner of the dog can be contacted.

Most dog tags are only valid for one year, and will need to be renewed annually at the beginning of every New Year, which involves paying a fee, which can vary from jurisdiction to jurisdiction.

From one extreme to the next, owners of dogs living in Beijing, China must pay a licensing fee of $600. (£360), while those living in Great Britain require no fee, because licensing of dogs was abolished in 1987.

Ireland and Northern Ireland both require dogs to be licensed and in Germany dog ownership is taxed, rather than requiring licensing, with higher taxes being paid for breeds of dogs deemed to be "dangerous".

Most US states and municipalities have licensing laws in effect and Canadian, Australian and New Zealand dogs also must be licensed, with the yearly fee approximately $30 to $50 (£18 to £30) depending upon whether the dog has been spayed or neutered.

## 10. Pet Insurance

Pet guardians commonly ask themselves, when considering medical insurance for their dog, whether they can afford *not* to have it.

## Chapter 12: Medical Care & Safety

On the one hand, in light of all the new treatments and medications that are now available for our dogs, that usually come with a very high price tag, an increasing number of guardians have decided to add pet insurance to their list of monthly expenses.

On the other hand, some humans believe that placing money into a savings account, in case unforeseen medical treatments are required, makes more sense.

Pet insurance coverage can cost anywhere from $2,000 to $6,000 USD (£1201 to £3604) over an average lifespan of a dog, and unless your dog is involved in a serious accident, or contracts a life-threatening disease, you may never need to pay out that much for treatment.

Whether you decide to start a savings account for your Teacup Yorkie so that you will always have funds available for unforeseen health issues, or you decide to buy a health insurance plan, most dog lovers will go to any lengths to save the life of their beloved companions.

Having access to advanced technological tools and procedures means that our dogs are now being offered treatment options that were once only reserved for humans.

Now, some canine conditions that were once considered fatal, are being treated at considerable costs ranging anywhere between $1,000. and $5,000. (£597. and £2,986.) or more.

However, even in the face of rapidly increasing costs of caring for our dogs, owners purchasing pet insurance remain a small minority.

In an effort to increase the numbers of people buying pet insurance, insurers have teamed with the American Kennel Club and Petco Animal Supplies to offer the insurance, and more than 1,600 companies, such as Office Depot and Google, offer pet

## Chapter 12: Medical Care & Safety

insurance coverage to their employees as an optional employee benefit.

Even though you might believe that pet insurance will be your savior anytime your dog needs a trip to the vet's office, you really need to be careful when considering an insurance plan, because there are many policies that contain small print excluding certain ages, hereditary or chronic conditions.

Unfortunately, most people don't consider pet insurance when their pets are healthy because buying pet insurance means playing the odds, and unless your dog becomes seriously ill, you end up paying for something that may never happen.

However, just like automobile insurance, you can't buy it after you've had that accident.

For instance, if you take your dog to your veterinarian who discovers that they have something wrong with their eyes, and then you decide to purchase insurance, because you will be required to give the insuring company a history of your dog's health, the eye issue will be part of the history and will likely be excluded from your insurance policy.

In other words, if you're planning on purchasing health insurance for your dog, do it before any problems arise in order to avoid having conditions that may present themselves in the future from being excluded from your policy.

As well, you need to keep in mind that canine health insurance rates will likely increase as your dog becomes older. When your dog is younger, while your policy may only be $17. (£10.) per month, it may increase considerably to as much as $170. (£100.) or more per month as your dog becomes middle or senior aged, at around 8 to 10 years of age.

Since many of us, in today's uncertain economy, may be hard pressed to pay a high veterinarian bill, generally speaking, the

## Chapter 12: Medical Care & Safety

alternative of paying monthly pet insurance premiums will provide peace of mind and improved veterinarian care for our best friends.

Shop around, because as with all insurance policies, pet insurance policies will vary greatly between companies and the only way to know for certain exactly what sort of coverage you are buying is to be holding a copy of that policy in your hand so that you can clearly read what will and what will not be covered.

Don't forget to carefully read the fine print to avoid any nasty surprises, because the time to discover that a certain procedure will not be covered is not when you are in the middle of filing a claim.

**Before Purchasing a Policy**

There are several considerations to be aware of before choosing to purchase a pet insurance policy, including:

- Is your dog required to undergo a physical exam?
- Is there a waiting period before the policy becomes active?
- What percentage of the bill does the insurance company pay — after the deductible?
- Are payments limited or capped in any way?
- Are there co-pays (cost to you up front)?
- Does the plan cover pre-existing conditions?
- Does the plan cover chronic or recurring medical problems?
- Can you choose any vet or animal hospital to treat your pet?
- Are prescription medications covered?
- Are you covered when traveling with your pet?
- Does the policy pay if your pet is being treated and then dies?

When you love your dog and worry that you may not have the funds to cover an emergency medical situation that could unexpectedly cost thousands, the right pet insurance policy will provide both peace of mind and better health care for your beloved fur friend.

## 11. Identifying and Finding Lost Dogs

### a) Micro-Chipping

A microchip implant is a very small integrated circuit, approximately twice the size of a grain of rice, enclosed in glass that is implanted underneath the dog's skin (or other animal) with a syringe.

The chip uses passive Radio Frequency Identification (RFID) technology, and is also known as a PIT tag (Passive Integrated Transponder).

The microchip is usually implanted, without anesthetic, into the scruff of a dog's neck by a veterinarian or shelter.

The microchip has no internal power source, which means that they must be read by a scanner or *"interrogator"* which energizes the capacitor in the chip, which then sends radio signals back to the scanner so that the identifying number can be read.

Manufacturers of microchips often donate scanners to animal shelters and veterinarian clinics and hospitals.

While many communities are proposing making micro-chipping of all dogs mandatory, such as N. Ireland, and micro-chipping is a requirements for any dogs traveling to the state of Hawaii, many others are not especially pleased with this idea because they believe it's just more big business for little reward.

For instance, while approximately one quarter of European dogs have a microchip implant, the idea is definitely lacking in popularity in the United States, where only 5% of dogs are micro-chipped.

## Chapter 12: Medical Care & Safety

Even though micro-chipping is used by animal shelters, pounds, animal control officers, breeders and veterinarians, in order to help return a higher percentage of lost canines to their owners, some of the resistance to this idea can be explained by inherent problems with the ability of some organizations to correctly read the implants.

As an example, if the scanner is not tuned to the same frequency as the implanted microchip, it will not be read, which renders the process useless.

Pet microchips are manufactured with different frequencies, including 125 kHz, 128 kHz and 134.2 kHz.

While approximately 98% of the pet microchips in the US use 125 kHz, those in Europe use 134.2 kHz.

In other words, if the facility reading your dog's microchip does not have a compatible scanner, your dog will not be identified and returned to you.

Further, what may turn out to be worse than the scanner incompatibility problem could be increasing evidence to indicate that microchips might cause cancer.

As well some microchips will migrate inside the dog's body and while they may start out in the dogs neck, they could end up in their leg or some other body part.

You will have to weigh information known about microchips, including possible cancer risks, and the odds of losing your dog against whether or not a microchip is something you want to have for your Teacup Yorkie.

Whether or not you choose a microchip for your dog, generally the cost ranges between $25 and $50 (£15 and £30) depending on what your veterinarian may charge for this service.

## Chapter 12: Medical Care & Safety

**b) Tattooing**

Dogs are tattooed to help identify them in case they are lost or stolen and many dog guardians prefer this safe, simple solution to micro-chipping.

Tattooing does not require locating a scanner that reads the correct frequency and there are no known side effects.

Because a tattoo is visible, it is immediately recognizable and reported when a lost dog is found, which means that tattooing could easily be the most effective means of identification available.

As well, dog thieves are less likely to steal a dog that has a permanent visible form of identification. There are several registries for tattooed dogs, including the National Dog Tattoo Registry in the UK, which has a network of Accredited Tattooists across the UK.

The fee for tattooing and registering a dog for their lifetime is approximately $42.52 (£24.98).

In the United States, the National Dog Registry (NDR) was founded in 1966 and since then, NDR has supervised, directed, conducted, or overseen the tattooing of more than 6 million animals.

The cost for tattooing a single dog is approximately $10 (£5.90), and you will also have to pay a one-time registration fee of $45 (£26.44).

**c) Where to Look**

If your Teacup Yorkie goes missing, there are many places you can contact and steps you can take that may help you locate your lost dog, including:

*Chapter 12: Medical Care & Safety*

- Retracing your dog's last known location;

- Contacting your friends and neighbours;

- Putting up flyers on telephone poles throughout your neighbourhood, with your contact details and a photograph of your dog;

- Calling all local shelters and pounds every day;

- Contacting local rescue organisations;

- Contacting your breeder;

- Contacting local schools -- children might have seen your dog in their neighbourhood;

- Distributing flyers with a photograph of your dog and your contact details in all neighbourhood stores and businesses;

- Contacting all businesses that deal with lost pets;

- Posting a picture on your Facebook or other social media;

- Asking your local radio station for help;

- Advertising in your local newspaper.

## 12. Yearly Cost of Ownership

It can be difficult to accurately estimate what the cost of owning every Teacup Yorkie might be because there are too many variables and unexpected medical problems, which might arise that may not otherwise be considered average.

For instance, you may like to buy fancy clothes, new collars and leashes every year, the latest toys and gadgets, or the most expensive food for your dog every week that might also not be considered average.

## Chapter 12: Medical Care & Safety

However, when thinking about sharing your life with a dog, it's important to consider more than just the daily cost of feeding your Teacup Yorkie.

Many humans do not think about whether or not they can truly afford to care for a dog before they bring one home, and not being prepared can cause stress and problems later on.

Remember that being financially responsible for your Teacup Yorkie is a large part of being a good guardian.

Beyond the initial investment of purchasing your Teacup Yorkie puppy from a reputable breeder, for most guardians, owning a Teacup Yorkie will include the costs associated with the following:

- Food
- Treats
- Pee pads, poop bags, potty patches
- Leashes and collars
- Safety harnesses
- Travel kennels or bags
- House training pens
- Clothing
- Toys
- Beds
- Professional grooming or equipment
- Shampoo and conditioner
- Neutering or spaying
- Regular veterinary care
- Obedience or dog whispering classes
- Pet sitting, walking or boarding
- Pet insurance
- Tattooing
- Micro-chipping
- Yearly licensing

## Chapter 12: Medical Care & Safety

- Unexpected emergencies

As you can see from the list above, there are many variables involved with being a canine guardian that may or may not apply to your particular situation.

For instance, depending upon where you shop, what type of food and how much you feed your Teacup Yorkie, what sort of veterinarian or grooming care you choose, whether or not you have pet insurance and what types of items you purchase for your Teacup Yorkie's well being, the yearly cost of owning a Teacup Yorkie could be estimated at anywhere between $700 and $3,000 (£420. and £1,800.).

Other contributing factors that may have an effect on the overall yearly cost of owning a Teacup Yorkie can include the region where you live, the weather, the accessibility of the items you need, your own lifestyle preferences and your Teacup Yorkie's age and individual needs.

**NOTE:** another interesting fact that may influence the overall cost associated with caring for a particular breed of dog is, according to a recent study of 2,000 dogs, closely related to what breed of dog you may be sharing your home with.

According to a recent article written by Sarah Griffiths and published in the Daily Mail on June 13, 2014, there is now a list of the top ten most *"destructive"* purebred dog breeds.

This interesting study was carried out in reference to damage a dog may cause by ripping up the carpet, chewing through the fence, destroying the plants in the garden, eating the remote or your most expensive shoes, etc.

Of course, all us humans expect some degree of damage from our furry friends during their lifetime, however, sometimes it can be quite a surprisingly large amount when you begin to add up the total amounts spent on cleaning, replacing and repairing damaged

*Chapter 12: Medical Care & Safety*

property, and the amount can be even higher if your dog becomes involved in destroying the neighbor's property, too.

The prize for the top ten destroyers is awarded to the cute and tiny Chihuahua, with average repair costs totaling $1,468. (£866) over the dog's lifetime, followed by the Dachshund, Dalmatian, Bulldog, Great Dane, Husky, Beagle, Pointer and German Shepherd.

On the other hand, the top ten <u>least destructive</u> breeds, in descending order, include such candidates as the Staffordshire Bull Terrier, causing a reported $302. (£178.) of damage over the dog's lifetime, followed by the West Highland White Terrier, Yorkshire Terrier, Spaniel, Whippet, Shih Tzu, Labrador, Jack Russell, Rottweiler and Sheepdog.

With all the cross breeding and creation of hybrid, designer canines these days, there are some very interesting studies being carried out, such as this one, that will help us humans better understand our favorite companions and what we may be letting ourselves in for.

**NOTE**: the more popular a particular breed may be, and the more positive traits a particular breed may enjoy will also make the cost of initially purchasing a puppy from a breeder more costly.

# Chapter 13: Coat Colors and Types

The American Kennel Club is very particular about coat coloration and even though a Yorkie with non-standard breed colors will still be permitted registration, they will not be permitted to compete in any AKC sponsored events.

## 1. Style

Breed standards for the Yorkie demand that the coat must be fine, straight, glossy and silky feeling.

A Yorkshire Terrier in traditional cut, as well as for show purposes, would have a long, grown out coat parted down the middle of the back. The length of the coat must never interfere with the dog's movement and can be just long enough to lightly kiss the floor.

## 2. Body Color

For showing purposes, the coat color, from the back of the neck to the base of the tail, should range in color from a dark gray to black, with the hair on the tail itself displaying a darker black.

On the head, show standards dictate that the hair on the chest and legs should be a bright, rich tan, darker at the roots than in the middle, that shades into a lighter tan at the tips.

Also, in adult dogs, there should be no dark hairs mixed in with any of the tan colored hair.

There are five categories of acceptable, standard breed colors for Yorkshire Terriers and these are the only coloring choices available on the American Kennel Club (AKC) application form for registering a Yorkshire Terrier.

## Chapter 13: Coat Colors and Types

These accepted colorings include: black and tan, black and gold, blue and gold, and blue and tan, and since the year 2000, particolored coats can also be registered.

Even though breeding and showing standards are very strict, adult Yorkshire Terriers that are born with coat colors outside of the standard, or that have extra fine or woolier coat textures are still considered to be Yorkies.

Dogs born with coat colors or textures considered to be atypical would not intentionally be bred as very fine coated or wooly coats can create more difficulty grooming.

**NOTE:** one of the more serious reasons given for not breeding Yorkshire Terriers that do not adhere to the standard color patterns, or who are considered *"off-colored"* Yorkies, is that an unusual color could be a potential indicator of a genetic defect that may affect the dog's health.

Therefore, careful and conscientious breeders will not wish to continue a breeding line that may perpetuate genetic defects.

If a puppy is born with an off-colored, wooly or very fine coat, careful veterinarian health screening can determine if any health risks exist and as they would not be considered show standard, the price for these puppies may be lower.

## 3. Puppy Coats

Newborn Yorkie puppies are born almost entirely black with tan points showing inside the ears, above the eyes, on the muzzle, around the legs, feet and toes, and the underside of the tail.

Occasionally a Yorkshire Terrier puppy may be born with a white "star" on the chest or displaying white below the mouth or on one or more toes.

## Chapter 13: Coat Colors and Types

Many breeders agree that a puppy born with a white mark on the chest will grow a long full coat when full grown. These white markings usually fade quickly and will have disappeared within a few short months. Also, some Yorkies can be born with a coat displaying a reddish tint and it is also common to find a white patch on one or more nails. These markings also fade with age, and have usually disappeared within a few months.

It may take two to three years or more for the Yorkshire Terrier coat to attain its final color, which means that when registering a dog, choosing a coloring for American Kennel Club (AKC) registration purposes will be a best guess for the new puppy owner. However, breeders who know their lines well should be able to fairly accurately predict the final adult coat coloring of their puppies, which will usually be a black/grayish color.

Although breed standards are always changing and new color combinations being accepted into registries, the show world can be somewhat testy about such seemingly insignificant details as coat color.

As an example, P. H. Combs, writing in the late 1800's, complained about show wins awarded to puppies (when the dog's coat does not fully come in until three or four years old) as follows:

*"... the honor of winning such a prize (for a puppy) can*

*Chapter 13: Coat Colors and Types*

*therefore be of but little practical benefit to the owner..."*

Many would agree with this comment since the adult dog's coat color cannot be exactly predicted when they are still a puppy.

## 4. Adult Coats

There is an enormous amount that can be said about a Yorkie's coat and if you are planning to show your dog you will want to become closely familiar with official breed standards.

The official coat standard for Yorkshire Terriers, which is dictated to the American Kennel Club (AKC) by the Yorkshire Terrier Club of America (YTCA), states that the coat must be glossy, fine, and silky, and also perfectly straight, being long on the face and moderately long on the body.

While you may not be so particular about the coat of your Teacup Yorkie, the approved breed standard is defined as *"perfection"* and it's this perfection that all responsible Yorkie breeders will work toward producing. Serious breeders will agree that any Yorkie that deviates anything more than very slightly from this standard coat color would not be considered breeding quality.

Of course, not every Yorkshire Terrier is born perfect because throwbacks can suddenly spring up out of genes from the original DNA of the dogs that were bred to create the breed, and since all three of the breeds believed to be responsible for the creation of the Yorkshire Terrier breed are now extinct, reliable information concerning the origins of the Yorkshire Terrier is, like most other purebred canines, questionable.

## 5. Coat Types & Colors

The coat standard for the Yorkie breed, consisting of the typical fine, straight, and silky coat, has been listed by many popular dog forums and information websites, as being hypoallergenic.

## Chapter 13: Coat Colors and Types

When compared to many other dog breeds, the Yorkshire Terrier is rated number three out of the top ten hypoallergenic breeds that are considered not to shed their hair or have excessive dander, and it's the dander and saliva that usually trigger most allergic reactions.

While allergists do recognize that differences in protein production between different dog breeds which may produce or alleviate symptoms in a particular allergy patient, they cannot agree that the luck of a few allergy sufferers, who might be able to tolerate a particular dog, can be stretched so far as to be true for all allergic humans and entire breeds of dogs.

However, the Yorkshire Terrier coat is noted to fall out only when brushed or broken, in the same manner as human hair will fall out.

### a) Cottony / Wooly Coats

Yorkies with cottony coats will usually show a profuse amount of hair from the time they are newborn puppies and as they grow, the hair continues to grow in length and bulk. Due to the bulkiness of this type of cotton or wooly coat, a Yorkie with a cotton or wooly coat may appear to be almost twice as large as they actually are.

Although a wooly or cottony-coated Yorkshire Terrier may well have the correct coat color and length, no matter how much you may fuss and groom, they will never attain the appearance of a silky-haired breed standard show dog.

### b) Wiry / Short / Red-Legged Coats

Red-legged Yorkies are also called wiry or shorter coated Yorkshire Terriers, and refer to dogs with hair that never grows long.

The coat length on these dogs can grow to be anywhere from two to six inches and everywhere in between with the hair on the face of a *"red-legged"* dog usually growing longer than the hair on the

## Chapter 13: Coat Colors and Types

body.

The legs tend to be very dark in color, with deep, rich tans that in natural light will appear almost reddish colored, while the black in the coat is a true black that rarely turns the traditional Yorkshire Terrier steel blue color. Some breeders say that this coat color is the result of those early Scots, who originally created the breed, and used red legged Yorkshire Terriers to add color and proper coat texture back into their breeding lines.

### c) Other Colors

Parti colors, (white with black/blue and tan) do exist, as do liver or chocolate colored Yorkies, although many are not considered correct for the breed standard because this purebred canine is defined by its color, and therefore, non-standard colors may indicate health problems or some sort of cross-breeding.

**Parti Color Coats:** it is quite rare to find a Yorkshire Terrier with a parti colored coat and if one is found, due to it's unique coloring or unusual color pattern, they will often be advertised at premium prices, as highly desirable, rare and exotic designer dogs.

Some Yorkshire Terriers are unable to produce the black pigment in their coat, and in this case will be a brown color referred to as liver or chocolate.

The American Kennel Club (AKC) registration form for Yorkshire Terriers has up until quite recently, when it permitted the registration of parti colored dogs in the year 2000, permitted only four choices: blue and tan, blue and gold, black and tan, black and gold.

Of course, color alone will have no affect upon whether or not a dog is a good companion and pet.

Although the American Kennel Club will not deny registration of a Yorkie based on color alone, the Yorkshire Terrier Club of

## Chapter 13: Coat Colors and Types

America has a directive which states that *"any solid color or combination of colors other than black and tan"* for adult dogs is a disqualification, and *"dogs of solid color, unusual combination of colors, and parti colors should be disqualified"* from showing in AKC sanctioned dog shows because of the white coloring.

**Piebald / Biewer Coats**: also called *"tri-colored", "banded"* or *"Biewer"* Yorkshire Terriers have been around for as long as the breed has existed and this coloration was considered a disqualification of the breed, which meant that breeders either destroyed puppies born with this color of coats or gave them away as pets.

With the dawning of the "designer" or "hybrid" dog" age, which has caused a great upsurge in owners becoming much more interested in unique colors and patterns, breeders have now also become more interested in the piebald coloring presented in the tri-colored or Biewer Yorkshire Terrier.

In 1984 a piebald Yorkie was born as a result of a genetic recessive gene occurrence from two German Yorkshire Terriers born at the Friedheck kennel.

Although much controversy remains today around the subject, the piebald dogs are considered a different breed in Germany because the German registrations would not admit the banded or tri colored Yorkies into their registry, even though registries in the United States do.

As a result of this registry discrimination, Germany formed a separate registry, which was given the breed name of *"Biewer Yorkshire Terrier à la Pom Pon"*.

Had the German Breed Club permitted the tri or banded colored Yorkie to be registered, then the Biewer Breed would not now exist and this type of coat coloration would instead be simply named "Tri Colored" Yorkshire Terriers.

## Chapter 13: Coat Colors and Types

Werner Biewer found the original piebald puppy to be quite beautiful and therefore began a selective breeding program to produce more piebald puppies.

As a result of his breeding efforts, the Biewer Yorkie was officially recognized, during the year 1986, by the Allgemeiner Club der Hundefreunde Deutschland (ACH).

Although there are many who will argue that the Biewer Yorkie is a separate breed, the original standard of the Biewer Yorkshire à la Pom-Pon is actually no different than that of any other Yorkshire Terrier, except for a different coat coloring.

After Mr. Werner Biewer passed away in 1997, Mrs. Biewer kept a few Biewer Yorkies as pets and the Friedheck kennel ceased to exist.

In the United States, owners purchasing tri colored puppies from the Nikkos kennels (the Lipmans), who were breeding champion Yorkshire Terriers, wanted their tri colored dogs registered with the American Kennel Club (AKC).

As these dogs were born from two purebred AKC registered dogs and they wanted the right color to be shown on the papers (Black, white and tan), in the year 2000, after 18 months of DNA testing, the AKC finally accepted the tri- colored Yorkshire Terrier into their registry.

Now, for piebald Yorkshire Terriers, AKC papers state that they are Yorkshire Terrier/Parti color on the papers, which means that the name *"parti Yorkies"* has stuck with the piebald, or tri color Yorkies.

As often happens when attempting to locate the original DNA of a particular canine, controversy and speculation still exists concerning the true lineage of the Biewer Yorkshire Terrier because the Biewers also raised Shih Tzu's, therefore there are

## Chapter 13: Coat Colors and Types

many who claim that the Biewer is a cross between a Yorkshire Terrier and a Shih Tzu.

While it is unlikely a piebald puppy would be born from a first generation Yorkie crossed with a Shih Tzu, this is possible if the Yorkshire Terrier's parents carried the piebald gene.

It has also been noted that the body conformation and coat texture, as well as the problem with the ears not standing erect in the Biewer Yorkshire Terrier could certainly result from pairing with a Shih Tzu.

Still others are convinced that the Maltese breed is responsible for the make-up of the piebald gene found in the Biewer Yorkie.

Unfortunately, whatever the true heritage of the Biewer Yorkshire Terrier may or may not be, it will never be confirmed one way or the other because DNA testing was not undertaken to determine parentage of the first presented Biewer Yorkshire Terrier.

The origin of the tri color pattern now hardly seems of consequence when tri colored, banded, piebald or Biewer Yorkshire Terriers can be found all around the world.

## 6. Tail Docking

Shortening a dog's natural tail length (also called *"shortening"* or *"bobbing"*, has become a hot topic of discussion over the years with many believing that the practice, which was originally carried out for practical and health related reasons, should be banned for all breeds. Opposition to the practice of docking tails or ears began very early in the history of the Yorkshire Terrier breed.

As early as 1878, Hugh Dalziel, who wrote about British dogs, declared of the Yorkshire Terrier that *"There is no reason for mutilating pet dogs, and perfect ears and tails should be bred, not clipped into shape with scissors."*

In the past, the Yorkshire Terrier tail has been customarily docked to a medium length and carried somewhat higher than the back.

Although shortened tails remain a breed standard, according to the American Kennel Club, there are other clubs that have relaxed this ruling to allow natural tails, especially in Belgium, Germany and Switzerland and most parts of Europe where the docking of tails is illegal.

When the Yorkie was a working dog, it made sense to dock their tails because they were hunting rodents and other burrowing animals that live in tunnels and therefore, docking their tails prevented the tail from getting broken or injured in tight spaces. Nowadays, many will agree that docking the tail has become nothing more than a cosmetic enhancement.

### a) Non-Surgical

When a puppy is only a few days old, docking the tails is a simple procedure that involves restricting circulation to the tail by tightly banding the tail by tying a rubber ligature around the puppy's tail very soon after it's born. Placing a band around the tail restricts blood flow to the end of the tail, which causes it to fall off within a couple of days.

### b) Surgical

The surgical procedure for shortening or docking the top portion of an older puppy's or dog's tail must be carried out by a licensed veterinarian surgeon and as this procedure will be more painful, they must be fully anesthetized.

## 7. Defining Features

Generally, the most distinctive features of a Teacup Yorkie will be its long, silky, blue gray, black and tan coat, and it's upright ears and small stature with a maximum weight size of 4 pounds (3.2 kilograms) or less.

# Chapter 14: Grooming

You will want to get your Teacup Yorkie puppy used to the routine of grooming early on, so that they will not be traumatized for the rest of their life, every time grooming is necessary.

Not taking the time to regularly involve your Teacup Yorkie puppy in grooming sessions could lead to serious, unwanted behavior that may include trauma to your dog, not to mention stress or injury to yourself in the form of biting and scratching, that could result in a lifetime of unhappy grooming sessions.

When you neglect regular, daily or at least a weekly at home grooming session with your puppy or dog to remove dead hair and check toenails, this will not only cost you and your canine companion, in terms of possible trauma it may also cost you in veterinarian fees should you not be aware of a problem that could have been discovered early on during regular grooming sessions.

An effective home regimen will depend on the length of your Teacup Yorkie's coat, and should include not just surface brushing, but also getting to all those sensitive areas easily missed around the ears and collar area, the armpit area, and the back end and tail.

Do not allow yourself to get caught in the *"my dog doesn't like it"* trap, which is an excuse many owners will use to avoid regular grooming sessions.

When you allow your dog to dictate whether they will permit a grooming session, you are setting a dangerous precedent that could lead to a lifetime of trauma for both you and your dog.

When humans neglect daily grooming routines, many dogs develop a heightened sensitivity, especially with regard to having their legs and feet held, their ears inspected, or their nails clipped, and will do anything they can to avoid the process when you need to groom them.

Make a pact with yourself right from the first day you bring your Teacup Yorkie puppy home, never to neglect a regular grooming routine and not to avoid sensitive areas, such as regular brushing, trimming toenails or brushing teeth, just because your dog may not particular *"like"* it.

Remember that a few minutes of regular grooming sessions each day with your Teacup Yorkie is also wonderful opportunity for closely bonding.

## 1. Bath Time

**Step One**: before you get your Teacup Yorkie anywhere near the water, it's important to make sure that you brush out any debris, dead hair, mats or tangles from their coat before you begin the bathing process.

As well, removing any debris or mats from your dog's coat beforehand will make the entire process easier on both you, your dog, and your drains, which will become clogged with dead hair if you don't remove it beforehand.

**Step Two**: if your Teacup Yorkie has a longer coat, the process will be much easier if you first spray the coat with a light mist of leave-in conditioner before brushing. This will also help to protect the hair strands against breakage.

**Step Three**: whether you're bathing your Teacup Yorkie in your laundry tub, bathtub or sink, you will always want to first lay down a rubber bath mat to provide a more secure footing for your dog and to prevent your tub or sink from being scratched.

**Step Four**: have everything you need for the bath (shampoo, conditioner, sponge, towels) right next to the sink or tub, so you don't have to go searching once your dog is already in the water.

**TIP:** place cotton balls in your Teacup Yorkie's ear canals to prevent accidental splashes from entering the ear canal that could later cause an ear infection.

**Step Five:** fill the tub or sink with four to six inches of lukewarm water (not too hot as dogs are more sensitive to hot water than us humans) and put your Teacup Yorkie in the water. Completely wet your dog's coat right down to the skin by using a detachable showerhead. If you don't have a spray attachment, a cup or pitcher will work just as well.

**TIP:** no dog likes to have water poured over its head and into its eyes, so use a wet sponge or wash cloth to wet the head area.

**Step Six:** apply shampoo as indicated on the bottle instructions by beginning at the head and working your way down the back. Be careful not to get shampoo in the eyes, nose, mouth or ears. Comb the shampoo lather through your dog's hair with your fingers, making sure you don't miss the areas under the legs and tail.

**Step Seven:** after allowing the shampoo to remain in your dog's coat for a couple of minutes, thoroughly rinse the Teacup Yorkie's coat, right down to the skin with clean, lukewarm water using the spray attachment, cup or pitcher. Comb through your dog's coat with your fingers to make sure all shampoo residue has been completely rinsed away.

**TIP:** any shampoo remaining in a dog's coat will lead to irritation and itching. Once you've rinsed, take the time to rinse again, especially in the armpits and underneath the tail area.

Use your hands to gently squeeze all excess water from your dog's coat.

**Step Eight:** apply conditioner as indicated on the bottle instructions and work the conditioner throughout your Teacup Yorkie's coat. Leave the conditioner in your dog's coat for two minutes and then thoroughly rinse again with warm water, unless the conditioner you are using is a *"leave-in"*, no-rinse formula.

**NOTE**: The best conditioner for a Teacup Yorkie will contain mink oil, which adds a gloss to deepen and enrich the natural color of the coat.

It is also a good idea to choose a brand of conditioner that contains sunscreen to help protect from ultraviolet radiation when your dog is outside on sunny days, and to protect their skin when they are clipped short.

Applying a good conditioner containing protein to your Teacup Yorkie's coat after bathing will help to rebuild, restructure and protect the coat by bonding to the shaft of each individual hair.

Pull the plug on your sink or tub and let the water drain away as you use your hands to squeeze excess water from your Teacup Yorkie's legs and feet.

**Step Nine**: immediately out of the water, wrap your Teacup Yorkie in dry towels so they don't get cold and use the towels to gently squeeze out extra water before you allow them to shake and spray water everywhere.

If your dog has longer hair, do not rub their coat with the towels, as this will create tangles and breakage in the longer hair.

Dry your Teacup Yorkie right away with your hand held hairdryer and be careful not to let the hot air get too close to their skin.

**TIP**: if your Teacup Yorkie's hair is longer, blow the hair in the direction of growth to help prevent breakage and if the hair is short, you can use your hand or a soft brush or comb to lift and fluff the coat to help it dry more quickly.

**TIP**: place your hand between the hairdryer and your Teacup Yorkie's hair so that they will never get a direct blast of hot air and never blow air directly into their face or ears.

Don't forget to remove the cotton balls from their ears.

## 2. Ear Care

There are many ear cleaning creams, drops, oils, rinses, solutions and wipes formulated for cleaning your dog's ears that you can purchase from your local pet store or veterinarian's office.

Or you may prefer to use a home remedy that will just as efficiently clean your Teacup Yorkie's ears, such as Witch Hazel or a 50:50 mixture of hydrogen peroxide and purified water.

**TIP**: if you are going to make your own ear cleaning solution, find a bottle with a nozzle, measure your solution, properly diluted and mixed into the bottle, and use your preparation to saturate a cotton makeup remove pad to wipe out the visible part of your dog's ears. Always make sure the ears are totally dried after cleaning.

## 3. Eye Care

Every dog should have their eyes regularly wiped with a warm, damp cloth to remove build up of daily secretions in the corners of the eyes that can be unattractive and uncomfortable for the dog as the hair becomes glued together.

If this build up is not removed every day, it can quickly become a cause of bacterial yeast growth that can lead to eye infections.

When you take a moment every day to gently wipe your dog's eyes with a warm, moist cloth, you will help to keep your dog's eyes comfortable and infection free.

## 4. Nail Care

Allowing your Teacup Yorkie to have long, untrimmed nails can result in various health hazards including infections or an irregular and uncomfortable gait that can result in damage to their skeleton.

Although most dogs do not particularly enjoy the process of having their nails trimmed, and most humans find the exercise to be a little scary, regular nail trimming is a very important grooming practice that should never be overlooked.

When you get them used to having their nails trimmed at a young age, they will quietly tolerate the process for the rest of their life.

In order to keep your adult Teacup Yorkie's toenails in good condition and the proper length, you will need to purchase a plier type nail trimmer at a pet store and learn how to correctly use it.

Generally speaking, if you can hear your dog's nails clacking or scratching on the floor or road surface when they walk, their nails are too long, and if you continue to allow your dog's nails to be too long, the nail quick will grow longer into the nail, which will make it more difficult to keep them trimmed to the correct length.

**NOTE**: when your Teacup Yorkie is a small puppy, it will be best to trim their nails with a pair of nail scissors, which you can purchase at any pet store, that are smaller and easier to use on puppy nails. All you need to do is snip off the curved tip of each nail.

Further, if you want your dog's nails to be smooth, without the sharp edges clipping alone can create, you will also want to invest in a toenail file or a special, slow speed, rotary Dremel™ trimmer, equipped with a sanding disk, which is designed especially for dog nails. Some dogs will prefer the rotary trimmer to the squeezing sensation of the nail clipper and when you keep your dog's nails regularly trimmed, the Dremel™ may be the only tool you will ever need.

**NOTE**: <u>never</u> use a regular Dremel™ tool on a dog's toenails as it will be too high speed and will burn your dog's toenails. Only use a slow speed Dremel™, Model 7300-PT Pet Nail Grooming Tool.

## 5. Dental Care

As a conscientious Teacup Yorkie guardian you will need to regularly care for your dog's teeth throughout their entire life.

**a) Retained Primary Teeth**

Often times a young dog will not naturally lose their puppy or baby teeth, especially those with small jaws, like the Teacup Yorkie, without intervention from a licensed veterinarian. Therefore, keep a close watch on your puppy's teeth around the age of 6 or 7 months of age to make certain that the baby teeth have fallen out and that the adult teeth have space to grow in. If your Teacup Yorkie puppy has not naturally lost all their baby teeth, any remaining teeth will need to be pulled, in order to allow room for the adult teeth to properly grow in, and the best time to do this will be at the same time they visit the veterinarian's office to be spayed or neutered.

**NOTE**: a smaller Teacup Yorkie will have a smaller jaw, which can result in more problems with teeth overcrowding.

An overcrowded mouth can cause teeth to grow unevenly or crooked and food and plaque to more easily build up, which will eventually result in bacterial growth on the surface of the teeth, causing bad breath, gum and dental disease.

**b) Periodontal Disease**

Please be aware that 80% of three-year-old dogs suffer from periodontal disease and bad breath because their guardians do <u>not</u> look after their dog's teeth.

## Chapter 14: Grooming

What makes this shocking statistic even worse is that with simple, daily care, it is possible to entirely prevent canine gum disease and bad breath.

The pain associated with periodontal disease will make your dog's life miserable, as it will be painful for them to eat and the associated bacteria can infect many parts of the dog's body, including the heart, kidney, liver and brain, all of which they will have to suffer in silence.

If your Teacup Yorkie has bad breath, this could be the first sign of an unhealthy mouth and gum disease caused by plaque build-up on the teeth.

As well, if your Teacup Yorkie is drooling excessively, this may be a symptom secondary to dental disease. Your dog may be experiencing pain or the salivary glands may be reacting to inflammation from excessive bacteria in the mouth.

If you notice your Teacup Yorkie drooling, you will want to have them professionally examined at your veterinarian's office.

### c) Teeth Brushing

Slowly introduce your Teacup Yorkie to teeth brushing early on in their young life so that they will not fear it.

Begin with a finger cap toothbrush when they are young puppies, and then move to a soft bristled toothbrush, or even an electric brush, as all you have to do is hold it against the teeth while the brush does all the work. Sometimes with a manual brush, you may brush too hard and cause the gums to bleed.

Never use human toothpaste or mouthwash on your dog's teeth because dogs cannot spit and human toothpaste that contains toxic fluoride will be swallowed. There are many flavored dog toothpastes available at the pet store or veterinarian's office.

## Chapter 14: Grooming

Also, it's a good idea to get your dog used to the idea of occasionally having their teeth scraped or scaled, especially the back molars which tend to build up plaque. Be very careful if you are doing this yourself because the tools are sharp.

**TIP**: if you need help keeping your dog's mouth open while you do a quick brush or scrape, get yourself a piece of hard material (rubber or leather) that they can bite down on, so that they cannot fully close their mouth while you work on their teeth.

When your Teacup Yorkie is a young puppy, take the time to get them used to having their mouth handled and your fingers rubbing their teeth and gums.

Next, buy some canine toothpaste at your local pet store specially flavored to appeal to dogs and apply this to your dog's teeth with your finger.

Then slowly introduce the manual or electric toothbrush to your Teacup Yorkie. When you go slowly, they will get used to the buzzing and vibrating of the electric brush, which will do a superior job of cleaning their teeth.

First, let them see the electric brush, then let them hear it buzzing, and before you put it in their mouth, let them feel the buzzing sensation on their body, while you move it slowly toward their head and muzzle.

When your Teacup Yorkie will allow you to touch their muzzle while the brush is turned on, the next step is to lift their lip and quickly brush a couple of teeth at a time until they get used to having them all brushed at the same time.

Always happily praise them for allowing you to brush their teeth, especially when they are first getting used to the idea.

**TIP:** another simple home solution for helping to keep your dog's breath fresh and their teeth white is Bicarbonate of Soda (baking soda). Simply sprinkle some into a dish and dip your finger or toothbrush first in water and then into the Bicarbonate of Soda. Then use this to clean your dog's teeth and massage their gums. Some dogs seem to object less to this procedure when you use your finger.

Whether you let the electric toothbrush do the work for you, or you are using your finger or a manual toothbrush, make certain that you brush in a circular motion and when using a brush, angle the bristles so that they extend underneath the gums to help prevent plaque buildup, gum disease and loose teeth.

### d) Teeth Scaling

Use of a tooth scraper or scaling tool once or twice a month can help to remove plaque buildup. Most accumulation will be found on the outside of the teeth and on the back molars, near the gum line.

Go slowly and carefully because these tools are sharp and only do this when your dog is calm and relaxed, a little bit at a time.

### e) Healthy Teeth Tips

Despite what most dog owners might put up with as normal, it is not normal for your dog to have smelly dog breath or canine halitosis.

Bad breath is the first sign of an unhealthy mouth, which could involve gum disease or tooth decay.

The following tips will help keep your Teacup Yorkie's mouth and teeth healthy:

## Chapter 14: Grooming

- Keep your dog's teeth sparkling white and their breath fresh by using old-fashioned hydrogen peroxide as your doggy toothpaste. Hydrogen peroxide is what's in the human whitening toothpaste. There will be such a small amount on the brush that it will not harm your dog, and will kill any bacteria in your dog's mouth.

- Many canine toothpastes are formulated with active enzymes to help keep tartar build-up at bay.

- Help prevent tooth plaque and doggy halitosis by feeding your dog natural, hard bones at least once a month, which will also help to remove tartar while polishing and keeping their teeth white.

- Feed large bones so there is no danger of swallowing, and do NOT boil the bones first because this makes the bone soft (which defeats the purpose of removing plaque), and boiling could cause bones to splinter into smaller pieces that could create a choking or puncturing hazard for your dog.

- Smaller dogs, such as the Teacup Yorkie, tend to be more vulnerable to teeth and gum problems, therefore, you really need to be brushing their teeth every single day.

- Feed a daily dental chew or hard biscuit to help to remove tartar while exercising jaws and massaging gums. Some dental chews contain natural breath freshening cinnamon, cloves or chlorophyll.

- Coconut oil also helps to prevent smelly dog breath while giving your dog's digestive, immune and metabolic functions a boost at the same time. Dogs love the taste, so add ¼ teaspoon to your Teacup Yorkie's dinner and their breath will soon be much sweeter.

Keep your Teacup Yorkie's mouth comfortable and healthy by getting into the habit of brushing their teeth every night before bedtime.

## 6. Skin Care

Keeping your Teacup Yorkie's coat clean by regularly bathing with canine shampoo and conditioner and free from mats, debris and parasites, as well as providing plenty of clean water and feeding them a high quality diet free from allergy-causing ingredients will go a long way toward keeping their skin healthy and itch-free and their coat shiny and healthy looking.

Between bath times, there are many moist doggy wipes on the market that are especially formulated with the correct pH balance to help keep your dog clean and their skin healthy. Consider getting into the habit of wiping down your dog with one of these moist towels every night before bed.

## 7. Pest Control

**Fleas**

Every dog usually picks up a flea or two sometime in their lifetime, so you should be prepared for this inevitability by ensuring that you have a good flea shampoo on hand as well as a flea comb.

If you notice your dog biting, scratching or chewing at his or herself, the chances that they have picked up a flea or two is quite high, so it's time for a flea bath.

**Ticks**

If your dog goes roaming freely through wooded and bushy areas with large trees, they may also pick up the occasional tick. Always carefully check through your dog's coat and ears after they have been romping through the woods, and make sure that

*Chapter 14: Grooming*

you also have a solution on hand that will kill a tick or the proper tool (a Tick Twister) that can easily and safely twist a tick out of a dog's skin.

A very effective product, which is 100% safe for humans and animals, that will also kill ticks and fleas on contact, is a natural pest control product called CedarCide.

As well, ticks can be quickly and easily removed with a simple to use *"Tick Twister"*.

## 8. Brushing and Combing

An often over looked task, that is a necessary part of maintaining the health of a Teacup Yorkie, is daily brushing and combing.

As well, taking time to brush and comb your Teacup Yorkie's coat will also give you an opportunity to bond with your dog, while identifying any problems (such as fatty lumps or bumps and matted hair) early on, before they may become more serious.

Make sure that your grooming sessions are as pleasant as possible by choosing the right tools for a Teacup Yorkie and their type and length of coat.

You will need minimal brushes and combs to keep your Teacup Yorkie's coat in good condition, including a slicker brush and a bristle brush.

## 9. Equipment Required

A **slicker brush** has short, thin, wire bristles arranged closely together and anchored to a flat, often rectangular, surface that's attached to a handle.

A slicker brush is an ideal grooming tool for helping to remove mats and tangles from a Teacup Yorkie who has a longer coat.

## Chapter 14: Grooming

Slicker brushes are often used as a finishing brush after brushing with the bristle brush to smooth the dog's coat and create a shiny finish.

A **bristle brush** can be used to help remove debris and dead hair from the coat and also to help distribute natural oils to keep the coat looking healthy and shiny.

A **metal comb** can also be used for grooming longer haired Teacup Yorkie. Most metal combs have a combination of widely spaced and narrow spaced teeth and are designed so that if you run into a tangle, you can switch to the wider spaced teeth while you work it out, without pulling and irritating your dog.

**NOTE**: Some combs have rotating teeth, which makes the process of removing tangles from your Teacup Yorkie's coat much easier on them without the pain of pulling and snagging.

**Mat splitters** are, as the name suggests, designed to split apart matted fur or hair so that you can then comb out the areas. Mats can quickly occur underneath the belly, in the armpits and tail area or around the neck.

**A rake** (which looks like a tiny rake) is very helpful for removing dead hair when your puppy is changing from their puppy coat to the new adult coat.

**Flea combs**, as the name suggests, are designed for the specific purpose of removing fleas from a dog's coat.

A flea comb is usually small in size for maneuvering in tight spaces, and may be made of plastic or metal with the teeth of the comb placed very close together to trap hiding fleas.

A **Tick Twister**, is a simple device for painlessly, easily and quickly removing ticks that have imbedded themselves in your dog's skin.

**Nail clippers** or scissors (and/or a slow speed pet Dremel™) will be tools you need to use every couple of weeks or more, depending on how quickly your dog's nails grow and what types of surfaces they may be walking on.

## 10. Products

### a) Shampoos

NEVER make the mistake of using human shampoo or conditioner for bathing your Teacup Yorkie because dogs have a different pH balance than humans.

For example, shampoo for humans has a pH balance of 5.5, whereas shampoo formulated for our canine companions has an almost neutral pH balance of 7.5.

Any shampoo with a lower pH balance will be harmful to your dog because it will be too harshly acidic for their coat and skin, which can create skin problems.

Always purchase a shampoo for your dog that is specially formulated to be gentle and moisturizing on your Teacup Yorkie's coat and skin, that will not strip the natural oils, and which will nourish your dog's coat to give it a healthy shine.

As a general rule, always read the instructions provided on the shampoo bottle, and avoid shampoos containing insecticides or harsh chemicals.

**TIP**: if your Teacup Yorkie is suffering from an infestation of fleas, you may want to bathe them with shampoo containing pyrethrum (a botanical extract found in small, white daisies) or a shampoo containing citrus or tea tree oil, or bath and spray them with the very effective CedarCide products which can also be used to spray down their bedding and any carpets in the home.

## b) Conditioners

While many of us humans use a conditioner after we shampoo our own hair, a large number of canine guardians forget to use a conditioner on our own dog's coat after bathing.

Even if the bathing process is one that you wish to complete as quickly as possible, you will want to reconsider this little oversight because, just as conditioning our human hair improves its condition, the same is true for our dog's coat.

Conditioning your Teacup Yorkie's coat will not only make it look and feel better, conditioning will also add additional benefits, including:

- Preventing the escape of natural oils and moisture;
- Keeping the coat cleaner for a longer period of time;
- Repairing a coat that has become damaged or dry;
- Restoring a soft, silky feel;
- Helping the coat dry more quickly;
- Protection from the heat of the dryer and breakage of longer coats during toweling, combing or brushing;

Spend the extra two minutes to condition your Teacup Yorkie's coat after bathing. The benefits of doing so will be appreciated by both yourself and your dog that will have overall healthy skin and a coat with a natural shine.

## c) De-tanglers

There are many de-tangling products you can purchase which will make the job of combing a longer coat much easier on both you and your Teacup Yorkie. De-tangling products work by making the hair slippery, and while some de-tanglers work well when used full strength, you may prefer a lighter, spray-in product.

As well, there are silicone products and grooming powders, or you can even use cornstarch to effectively lubricate the hair to help with removing mats and tangles before bathing.

**d) Styptic Powder**

You will always want to avoid causing any pain when trimming your Teacup Yorkie's toenails, because you don't want to destroy their trust in you by regularly performing this necessary task.

However, accidents do happen, therefore if you accidentally cut into the vein in the toenail, know that you will cause your dog pain, and that the toenail will bleed.

Therefore, it is always a good idea to keep some styptic powder (often called *"Kwik Stop"*) in your grooming kit. Dip a moistened finger into the powder and apply it to the end of the bleeding nail.

The quickest way to stop a nail from bleeding is to immediately apply styptic powder and firm pressure for a few seconds.

**TIP**: if you do not have styptic powder available, there are several home remedies that can help stop the bleeding, including a mixture of baking soda and cornstarch, or simply cornstarch alone. Also, a cold, wet teabag or rubbing with scent-free soap can also be effective. These home remedies will not be as instantly effective as styptic powder.

**e) Ear Powders**

Ear powders, which can be purchased at any pet store, are designed to help keep your dog's ears dry while at the same time inhibiting the growth of bacteria that can lead to infections. Ear powders are also used when removing excess hair growth from inside a dog's ear canal as the powder makes it easier to grip the hair.

## f) Ear Cleaning Solutions

Your local pet store will offer a wide variety of ear cleaning creams, drops, oils, rinses or wipes specially formulated for cleaning your dog's ears. As well, there are also many home remedies that will just as efficiently clean your dog's ears without the high price tag.

**NOTE**: because a dog's ears are a very sensitive area, always read the labels before purchasing products and avoid any solutions that list alcohol as the main ingredient.

## g) Home Ear Cleaning Solutions

The following are three effective home solutions that will efficiently clean your dog's ears:

> **Witch Hazel** is a natural anti-inflammatory that works well to cleanse and protect against infection while encouraging faster healing of minor skin traumas.
>
> A 50:50 solution of **Organic Apple Cider Vinegar and Purified Water** has been used as an external folk medicine for decades. This mixture is a gentle and effective solution that kills germs while naturally healing.
>
> A 50:50 solution of **Hydrogen Peroxide and Purified Water** is useful for cleansing wounds and dissolving earwax.

Whatever product you decide to use for cleaning your dog's ears, always be careful about what you put into your dog's ears and thoroughly dry them after cleaning.

## h) Canine Toothpastes

When it comes time to brush a dog's teeth, this is where many guardians fail miserably, often using the excuse that ***"my dog doesn't like it"***.

Whether they like it or otherwise is not the issue, because in order to keep your Teacup Yorkie healthy, they <u>must</u> have healthy teeth and the only way to ensure this, is to brush their teeth every day.

The many canine toothpastes on the market are usually flavored with beef or chicken in an attempt to appeal to the dog's taste buds, while others may be infused with mint or some other breath freshening ingredient in an attempt to appeal to humans by improving the dog's breath.

Honestly, your dog is not going to be begging for you to brush his or her teeth no matter how tasty the paste might be, therefore, effectiveness, in the shortest period of time, will be more of a deciding factor than whether or not your dog prefers the taste of the toothpaste.

Some dog toothpastes contain baking soda, which is the same mild abrasive found in many human pastes, and is designed to gently scrub the teeth. However, just how much time you will have to spend scrubbing your dog's teeth, before they've had enough, may be too minimal to make these pastes very effective.

Other types of canine toothpastes are formulated with enzymes that are designed to work chemically by breaking down tartar or plaque in the dog's mouth. These pastes do not need to be washed off your dog's teeth and are safe for them to swallow. Whether or not they remain on the dog's teeth long enough to do any good might be debatable.

**TIP**: old-fashioned hydrogen peroxide cleans while killing germs and keeping teeth white. Just dip your dog's toothbrush in a

## Chapter 14: Grooming

capful of hydrogen peroxide, shake off the excess, and brush their teeth. There will be such a small amount in your dog's mouth that you don't need to worry about them swallowing it.

**i) Paw Creams**

Depending upon the types of surfaces our canine counterparts usually walk on, they may suffer from cracked or rough pads. You can restore resiliency and keep your Teacup Yorkie's paws in healthy condition by regularly applying a cream or lotion to protect their paw pads.

**TIP**: a good time to do this is just after you have clipped their nails.

**NOTE**: if you live in a hot climate, be aware that sidewalks, road surfaces and sandy beaches can get extremely hot for your dog's feet. As well, a smaller sized Teacup Yorkie is that much closer to the hot surface, which means that on a hot day, they will be feeling the effects of being heated from both sides. If you live in a very hot climate, choose to walk them during the cooler hours of the day, walk them on grassy areas only, or carry them.

**j) Organic Pest Control**

CedarCide is a 100% safe, organic way to control biting bugs on your fur friends without worrying about harmful chemicals that are not good for you, your children or your canine companions. Simply spray it on, and bugs of any sort that come into contact with the solution will be dead, while your dog will smell like the inside of a cedar chest.

## 11. Professional Grooming

If you decide that you are not interesting in buying all the equipment (electric clippers, blades, scissors, nail clippers, combs, brushes, table, etc.) or enrolling yourself in a $4,000 (£2,388) course to learn how to professionally groom your Teacup Yorkie

## Chapter 14: Grooming

yourself, you will want to locate a trusted professional service to do this for you.

The best way to find a groomer is to ask others who they use and whether they are happy with the results.

If you have decided to keep your Teacup Yorkie clipped short, you will need to take them for a full grooming session approximately every 6 to 8 weeks.

An average price for professionally grooming a Teacup Yorkie will usually start around $60 (£40) and could be considerably more depending upon the size of the dog and whether the salon is also bathing and trimming nails.

# Chapter 15: Socializing

Most Teacup Yorkies are naturally friendly and social dogs, however, they will still need to be exposed to different people, places and unusual sights and sounds when they are puppies.

Any dog that is not regularly socialized may become shy or suspicious of unfamiliar or unusual people or circumstances, which could lead to nervous or fearful behavior.

## 1. With Other Dogs and Pets

Generally speaking, the majority of an adult dog's habits and behavioral traits will be formed between the ages of birth and one year of age.

This is why it will be very important to introduce your Teacup Yorkie puppy to a wide variety of locations, sights, sounds, smells and situations during this formative period in their young life.

Your Teacup Yorkie puppy will learn how to behave, in all these various circumstances, by following your lead, feeling your energy and watching how you react in every situation.

For instance, never accidentally reward your Teacup Yorkie puppy or dog for displaying nervousness, fear or growling at another dog or person by picking them up.

Picking up a Teacup Yorkie puppy or dog at this time, when they are displaying unbalanced energy, actually turns out to be a reward for them, and you will be teaching them to continue with this type of behavior.

As well, picking up a puppy places them in a top dog position, where they have the higher ground and literally (because they are

## Chapter 15: Socializing

higher up) become more dominant than the person or dog they may have just growled at.

The correct action to take in such a situation is to gently correct your Teacup Yorkie puppy, with a firm, yet calm energy by distracting them with a "no", or a quick sideways snap of the leash to get their attention back on you, so that they learn to let you deal with the situation on their behalf.

If you allow a fearful, nervous or shy puppy deal with situations that unnerve them without your direction, they may learn to react with fear or aggression to unfamiliar circumstances and you will have created a problem that could escalate into something more serious as they grow older.

The same is true of situations where a young puppy may feel the need to protect itself from a larger or older dog that may come charging in for a sniff.

It is the guardian's responsibility to protect the puppy so that they do not feel that they must react with fear or aggression in order to protect themselves.

Once your Teacup Yorkie puppy has received all their vaccinations, you can take them out to public dog parks and various locations where many dogs and people are found.

Before allowing them to interact with other dogs or puppies, take them for a disciplined walk on leash so that they will be a little tired and less likely to immediately pounce excitedly on all other dogs.

Keep your puppy on leash and close beside you, because most young puppies are a bundle of out of control energy, and you need to protect them while teaching them how far they can go before they may get themselves into trouble with adult dogs that might not appreciate their excited playfulness.

## Chapter 15: Socializing

Remember that they may not have experienced the company of other dogs since you brought them home, and now that they have completed their course of vaccinations, they will understandably be excited and perhaps a little hesitant about seeing dogs again.

Keep a close watch on your Teacup Yorkie puppy to make sure they are not being overwhelmed by too many other dogs, or getting overly excited and stressed or nervous, because it is your job to protect your puppy.

If your puppy shows any signs of aggression or domination toward another puppy, dog or person, you must immediately step in and calmly discipline them, otherwise by doing nothing, you will be agreeing with their behavior and will be allowing them to get into situations that could become serious behavioral issues as they grow in age and size.

No matter the age or size of your Teacup Yorkie puppy, allowing them to display aggression or domination over another dog or person is never a laughing matter and this type of behavior must be immediately curtailed.

## 2. With Other People

Take your puppy everywhere with you and introduce them to many different people of all ages, sizes and ethnicities.

This will be easy to do, because most people will automatically be drawn to you when they see you have a puppy because few humans can resist a puppy, especially one as cute as a Teacup Yorkie.

Most humans will want to interact with your puppy and if they ask to hold your puppy, this is a good opportunity to socialize your puppy and show them that humans are friendly.

Do not let others (especially young children) play roughly with your puppy or squeal at them in a high-pitched voices because this can be very frightening for a sensitive young puppy, such as the Teacup Yorkie.

As well, you do not want to teach your puppy that humans are a source of crazy, excited energy.

Be especially careful when introducing your puppy to young children who may accidentally hurt your puppy, because you don't want your dog to become fearful of children as this could lead to aggression issues later on in life.

Explain to children that your Teacup Yorkie puppy is very young and that they must be calm and gentle when playing or interacting in any way.

## 3. Within Different Environments

It can be a big mistake not to take the time to introduce your Teacup Yorkie puppy to a wide variety of different environments because when they are not comfortable with different sights and sounds, this could cause them possible trauma later in their adult life.

Be creative and take your puppy everywhere you can imagine when they are young so that no matter where they travel, whether strolling along a noisy city sidewalk or beside a peaceful shoreline, they will be equally comfortable.

Do not make the mistake of only taking your Teacup Yorkie puppy into areas where you live and will always travel because they need to also be comfortable visiting areas you might not often visit, such as noisy construction sites, airports or a shopping area across town.

Your puppy needs to see all sorts of sights, sounds and situations so that they will not become fearful should they need to travel with you to any of these areas.

## Chapter 15: Socializing

Your Teacup Yorkie puppy will take their cues from you, which means that when you are calm and in control of every situation, they will learn to be the same because they will trust your lead.

For instance, put your puppy in their Sherpa bag and take them to the airport where they can watch people and hear planes landing and taking off.

Take them to a local park where they can see a baseball game, or for a stroll beside a schoolyard at recess time when noisy children are out playing, or take them to the local zoo or farm and let them get a close up look at horses, pigs and ducks.

## 4. Loud Noises

Many dogs can show extreme fear of loud noises, such as fireworks or thunderstorms.

If you take the time to desensitize your Teacup Yorkie to these types of noises when they are very young, it will be much easier on them during stormy weather or holidays such as Halloween or New Year's when fireworks are often a part of the festivities.

You can purchase CD's that are a collection of unusual sounds, such as vacuums or hoovers, airplanes, people clapping hands, screaming children, and more, that you can play while working in your kitchen or relaxing in your living room or lounge.

When you play these sounds and pretend that everything is normal, the next time your puppy or dog hears these types of sounds elsewhere, they will not become upset or agitated because they have learned to ignore them.

Also make sure that you get your young puppy used to the sounds of thunder and fireworks at an early age because these types of shrieking, crashing, banging and popping sounds of fireworks or thunder as well as the high pitched beeping of household smoke and fire alarms can be so traumatic and unsettling for many dogs,

## Chapter 15: Socializing

that sometimes, no matter how much you try to calm your dog, or pretend that everything is fine, there is little you can do.

Some dogs literally lose their minds when they hear the loud popping or screeching noises of fireworks and alarms and start running or trying to hide and you cannot communicate with them at all.

Make sure that your dog cannot harm itself trying to escape from these types of noises, and if possible, calmly hold them until they begin to relax.

If your dog loses it's mind when it hears these types of noises, simply avoid taking them anywhere near fireworks and if at times when they might hear these noises going off outside, play your inside music or TV louder than you might normally, to help disguise the exterior noise of fireworks or thunder.

As well, some dogs will respond well to wearing a *"ThunderShirt"* which is specifically designed to alleviate anxiety or trauma associated with loud rumbling, popping or banging noises.

The idea behind the design of the ThunderShirt is that the gentle pressure it creates is similar to a hug that, for some dogs, has a calming effect.

Do not underestimate the importance of taking the time to continually (not just when they are puppies) socialize and desensitize your puppy to all manner of sights, sounds, individuals and locations because to do so will be teaching them to be a calm and well balanced member of your family that will quietly follow you in every situation.

# Chapter 16: Training

## 1. Trainability

As the Teacup Yorkie is an active small dog, they will almost undoubtedly love to participate in canine sports, such as Agility, and will be an intelligent and easy to train dog.

Many Yorkshire Terriers have earned the undeserved reputation of being noisy, irritating, *"yappy"* little dogs when in fact this breed is affectionate, intelligent and obedient when properly trained.

The behavioral problems begin to arise when the human guardians of this toy breed start to baby the dog, no longer respect it as a dog, and instead constantly carry it around and treat it like a small and precious fur child.

Every dog must have a leader, and if the humans that adopt the dog do not provide this leadership role for their Yorkie, then the dog will be forced to be the leader and this is when all sorts of troubles can start to bubble to the surface.

If you do not ensure that you are your dog's leader, the Yorkshire Terrier, no matter what their size, will become nervous and suspicious of strangers and other dogs to the point of even becoming aggressive if another dog or person comes near.

Every Yorkie guardian needs to be very aware that unless they provide rules and boundaries and a strong leadership role, these tenacious little terriers will truly take over and become territorial, loudly demanding and wholly obnoxious as they slip into the role of *"small dog syndrome"* and your friends stop visiting.

When taught with positive reinforcement, this tiny dog will be an eager learner who will easily excel at anything you have the time and patience to teach.

No matter what you decide to teach your Teacup Yorkie, always train with patience and kindness and NEVER yell, hit or punish a dog during training, or at any time for that matter.

Using harsh, mean or loud training methods could frighten a Teacup Yorkie and cause them to shut down.

As well, any sort of harsh treatment will cause your friendly and sensitive Teacup Yorkie to lose trust and respect of you, and they could also learn to fear you, which is NOT the type of relationship you want to have with your dog.

All training sessions should be happy and fun filled with plenty of rewards and positive reinforcement, which will ensure that your Teacup Yorkie is an excellent student who looks forward to learning new commands and tricks.

The Teacup Yorkie can be highly skillful in many different forms of advanced dog sports, including Agility, Obedience, Freestyle Dance, and more.

## 2. Puppy Training Basics

Most humans believe that they need to take their young dog to puppy classes, and generally speaking, this is a good idea for any young Teacup Yorkie (after they have had all their vaccinations), because it will help to get them socialized.

## Chapter 16: Training

Beyond puppy classes for socializations reasons, hiring a professional dog whisperer for personalized private sessions to train the humans may be far more valuable than training situations where there are multiple dogs and humans together in one class as this can be very distracting for everyone concerned.

### a) Three Most Important Words

**"Come"**, **"Sit"** and **"Stay"** will be the three most important words you will ever teach your Teacup Yorkie puppy.

These three basic commands will ensure that your Teacup Yorkie remains safe in almost every circumstance.

For instance, when your puppy correctly learns the "Come" command, you can always quickly bring them back to your side if you should see danger be approaching.

When you teach your Teacup Yorkie puppy the "Sit" and "Stay" commands you will be further establishing your leadership role. A puppy that understands that their human guardian is their leader will be a safe and happy follower.

### b) Choosing a Discipline Sound

Choosing a *"discipline sound"* that will be the same for every human family member will make it much easier for your puppy to learn what they can or cannot do and will be very useful when warning your Teacup Yorkie puppy before they engage in unwanted behavior.

The best types of sounds are short and sharp so that you and your family members can quickly say them and so that the sound will immediately get the attention of your Teacup Yorkie puppy because you want to be able to easily interrupt them when they are about to make a mistake.

*Chapter 16: Training*

It doesn't really matter what the sound is, so long as everyone in the family is consistent.

A sound that is very effective for most puppies and dogs is a simple **"UH"** sound said sharply and with emphasis.

Most puppies and dogs respond immediately to this sound and if caught in the middle of doing something they are not supposed to be doing will quickly stop and give you their attention or back away from what they were doing.

## 3. Beginner Leash Lesson

Equipment: 4 or 6-foot leash, Martingale training collar.

The most important ongoing bonding exercise you will experience with your new Teacup Yorkie puppy is when you go out for your daily walks together.

Far, far too many people ignore this critical, multi-tasking time that is not only important for your puppy's exercise, it fulfills a multitude of their needs, including:

- Exercising their body
- Fulfilling their natural roaming urges
- Teaching them discipline, which engages their mind
- Learning to follow, trust and respect you
- Reinforcing that you are their leader

As soon as you bring your new puppy home you will want to teach them how to walk at your side while on leash without pulling.

Every time your puppy needs to go out to relieve his or herself, slip on their collar and snap on that leash.

At first your Teacup Yorkie puppy may struggle or fight against having a collar around their neck, because the sensation will be

## Chapter 16: Training

new to them. However, at the same time they will want to go with you, so exercise patience and encourage them to walk with you.

Be careful never to drag them, and if they pull backward and refuse to walk forward with you, simply stop for a moment, while keeping slight forward tension on the leash, until your Teacup Yorkie puppy gives up and moves forward. Immediately reward them with your happy praise, and if they have a favorite treat, this can be an added incentive when teaching them to walk on their leash.

Always walk your puppy on your left side with the leash slack so that they learn that walking with you is a relaxing experience. Keep the leash short enough so that they do not have enough slack to get in front of you.

If they begin to create tension in the leash by pulling forward or to the side, simply stop moving, get them back beside you, and start over.

Be patient and consistent with your puppy and very soon they will understand exactly where their walking position is and will walk easily beside you without any pulling or leash tension.

Remember that walking with a new puppy is an exciting experience for them as they will want to sniff everything and explore their new world, so give them lots of understanding and don't expect them to be perfect all the time.

When your Teacup Yorkie puppy is very young, and wanting to put everything in their mouths, walk them in a harness AND collar and leash, so that you can have a second leash attached to the harness.

All puppies want to put everything in their mouths, therefore, when they are wearing a collar and leash, AND a harness and leash, you will be able to easily lift them over cigarette butts or other garbage you may encounter while out walking.

# Chapter 16: Training

Once they grow out of the habit of tasting all manner of garbage, you can dispense with the harness and second leash.

## 4. Surviving Adolescence

The adolescent period in a young Teacup Yorkie's life, between the ages of 6 and 12 months, is the transitional stage of both physical and psychological development when they are physically almost full grown in size, yet their minds are still developing and they are testing their boundaries and the limits that their human counterparts will endure.

This can be a dangerous time in a puppy's life because this is when they start to make decisions on their own which, if they do not receive the leadership they need from their human guardians, can lead to developing unwanted behaviors.

Learning how to make decisions on their own would be perfectly normal and desirable if your Teacup Yorkie puppy was living in the wild, amongst a pack of dogs, because learning to make decisions would be necessary for their survival.

However, when living within a human environment, your puppy must always adhere to human rules and it will be up to their human guardians to continue their vigilant, watchful guidance in order to make sure that they do.

Many humans are lulled into a false sense of security when their new Teacup Yorkie puppy reaches the age of approximately six months, because the puppy has been well socialized, they have been to puppy classes and long since been house trained.

The real truth is that the serious work is only now beginning and the humans and their new Teacup Yorkie puppy could be in for a time of testing that could seriously challenge the relationship and leave the humans wondering if they made the right decision to share their home with a dog.

## Chapter 16: Training

If the human side of the relationship is not prepared for this transitional time in their young dog's life, their patience may be seriously tried, and the relationship of trust and respect that has been previously built can be damaged, and could take considerable time to repair.

While not all adolescent puppies will experience a noticeable adolescent period of craziness, because every puppy is different, most young dogs do commonly exhibit at least some of the usual adolescent behaviors, including reverting to previous puppy behaviors.

Some of these adolescent behaviors might include destructive chewing of objects they have previously shown no interest in, selective hearing or ignoring previously learned commands, displaying aggressive behavior, barking uncontrollably, jumping on everyone, barking at everything that moves, or reverting to relieving themselves in the house, even though they were house trained months ago.

Keeping your cool and recognizing these adolescent signs is the first step toward helping to make this transition period easier on your Teacup Yorkie puppy and all family members.

The first step to take that can help keep raging hormones at bay, is to spay or neuter your Teacup Yorkie puppy just prior to the onset of adolescence, at around four or five months of age.

While spaying or neutering a Teacup Yorkie puppy will not entirely eliminate the adolescent phase, it will certainly help and at the same time will spare your puppy the added strain of both the physical and emotional changes that occur during sexual maturity.

As well, some female puppies will become extremely aggressive toward other dogs during a heat, and non-neutered males may become territorially aggressive and pick fights with other males.

*Chapter 16: Training*

Once your Teacup Yorkie puppy has been spayed or neutered, you will want to become more active with your young dog, both mentally and physically by providing them with continued and more complex disciplined exercises.

This can be accomplished by enrolling your adolescent Teacup Yorkie in a dog whispering session or more advanced training class, which will help them to continue their socialization skills while also developing their brain.

Even though it may be more difficult to train during this period, having the assistance of a professional and continuing the experience of ongoing socialization amongst other dogs of a similar size can be invaluable, as this is the time when many young dogs begin to show signs of antisocial behavior with other dogs as well as unknown humans.

When your Teacup Yorkie is provided with sufficient daily exercise and continued socialization with unfamiliar dogs, people and places that provides interest and expands their mind, they will be able to transition through the adolescent stage of their life much more seamlessly.

## 5. Releasing Energy

The adolescent period in any puppy's life is a time of boundless energy. Excess energy will be even more apparent in an intelligent, high energy Teacup Yorkie puppy and you will need to find ways to safely allow them to release this energy every day.

Since most humans cannot walk nearly fast enough to accommodate the needs of an energetic puppy, you will first want to walk your Teacup Yorkie beside you on leash, and then find a safe place where they can run off leash, either chasing a ball, retrieving a Frisbee or playing and running in an enclosed area with other similar sized dogs where you can always supervise.

## 6. The Unruly Adolescent

If your Teacup Yorkie puppy happens to be especially unruly during their adolescent phase, you will need to simply limit their opportunities for making mistakes.

For instance, a puppy who is digging up the yard, or chewing up just about anything they can get their teeth on will need to be closely supervised so that you can direct their energy into less harmful pursuits.

It does absolutely no good to yell at your Teacup Yorkie puppy for engaging in behavior you are not happy with, and in fact, yelling or getting angry will only desensitize your young dog from listening to any of your commands.

Further, although you may eventually get the results you want, if you yell loud enough, your puppy will then be reacting out of fear, rather than respect, and this will be damaging to your relationship.

Displaying calm, yet assertive energy is the ONLY energy that works well to help your adolescent puppy understand what is required of them.

All other human emotions (frustration, anger, impatience, sadness, excitement) are "read" by puppies and dogs as being unstable, and not only will the smart and sensitive Teacup Yorkie not understand these emotions, they will not respect you for displaying these types of unstable energies.

An extremely rambunctious adolescent Teacup Yorkie may need to have their free run of the house curtailed so that they are confined to areas where you can easily supervise them.

Make sure they are within eyesight at all times, so that if they do find an opportunity to make a mistake, you can quickly show them what is permitted and what is not.

## Chapter 16: Training

Adolescence may also be a time when you might have to insist that your young Teacup Yorkie sleeps in their crate with the door closed whenever you cannot supervise, as well as at bedtime so they continue to understand that you have firm rules.

As well, keeping on top of house training is also a good idea during the adolescent period of your puppy's life because some adolescent puppies may become stubborn and forget that they are already house trained.

This means actually taking the time to be involved in the process by leashing up your dog and physically taking them outside whenever they need to relieve themselves.

Many times humans that have back yards tend not to be very involved in the housebreaking routine because they just open a door and let their dogs run free in the back yard.

Too many humans with convenient yards simply do not participate at all in the bathroom routine of their young dogs and thereby miss out on endless opportunities to reinforce who is the boss.

### 7. Rewarding Unwanted Behavior

Often humans make the mistake of accidentally rewarding unwanted behaviors.

It is very important to recognize that any attention paid to an overly excited, out of control, adolescent puppy, even negative attention, is likely going to be rewarding for your puppy.

Therefore, when you engage with an out of control Teacup Yorkie puppy, you end up actually rewarding them, which will encourage them to continue more of this unwanted behavior.

Be aware that chasing after a puppy when they have taken something they are not supposed to have, picking them up when

## Chapter 16: Training

they are barking or showing aggression, pushing them off when they jump on you or other people, or yelling when they refuse to come when called, are all forms of attention that can actually be rewarding for most puppies.

As your Teacup Yorkie's guardian, it will be your responsibility to provide calm and consistent structure for your puppy, which will include finding acceptable and safe ways to allow your puppy to vent their energy without being destructive or harmful to property, other dogs, humans, or the actual puppy.

Activities that create or encourage an overly excited Teacup Yorkie puppy, such as rough games of tug-o-war, or wild games of chase through the living room, should be immediately curtailed, so that your adolescent puppy learns how to control their energy and play quietly and appropriately without jumping on everyone or engaging in barking or mouthy behavior.

Further, if your adolescent Teacup Yorkie puppy displays excited energy simply from being petted by yourself, your family members or any visitors, you will need to teach yourself, your family and your friends to ignore your puppy until they calm down. Otherwise, you will be teaching your Teacup Yorkie puppy that the touch of humans means excitement.

For instance, when you continue to engage with an overly excited puppy, you are rewarding them for out of control behavior and literally teaching them that when they see humans, you want them to display excited energy.

Worse, once your puppy has learned that humans are a source of excitement, you will then have to work very long and hard to reverse this behavior.

Children are often a source of excitement that can cause an adolescent puppy to be extremely wound up.

*Chapter 16: Training*

Do not allow your children to engage with an adolescent Teacup Yorkie puppy unless you are there to supervise and teach the children appropriate and calm ways to interact with the puppy.

In order to keep everyone safe, it is very important that your Teacup Yorkie puppy learn at an early age that neither children nor adults are sources of excitement.

You can help develop the mind of an adolescent Teacup Yorkie and the minds of growing children at the same time by teaching children that your puppy needs structured walks and by showing them how to play fetch, search, hide and seek, or how to teach the Teacup Yorkie puppy simple tricks and obedience skills that will be fun and positive interaction for everyone.

## 8. Back to Basics

When your puppy is going through what could be a belligerent and trying adolescence, when it seems that they have forgotten everything they may have learned so far, this is an especially good time to revisit the simple "Sit" command.

Now, in order to help re-establish your leadership role, you will want to ask your Teacup Yorkie puppy to sit at every opportunity.

The simple act of "sitting" will help to calm an excited mind and will get your puppy's focus back on you.

## 9. Sit and More Sit

Every time you take your Teacup Yorkie out for a walk, which is usually a cause of excitement, get into the habit of asking them to sit while you put on their leash — then ask them to sit and calmly wait while you put on your shoes or jacket — after you approach the door, ask them to sit again while you open the door — after you are on the other side of the door — ask them to sit again while you lock the door.

If there are stairs or landings involved, ask them to sit at the top and also again at the bottom.

Every time you arrive at street intersection or a crosswalk, ask your Teacup Yorkie puppy to sit again, and do this in reverse when coming back home.

Also, every time you stop during your walk to speak to a neighbor, greet a friend or admire the view, ask your puppy to sit.

Every time you ask your young dog to sit for you, they are learning several things all at once — that they must remain calm, that you are the boss and that they must respect you as their leader.

Also, a sitting puppy is much more easy to control than one standing at the alert, ready to bolt out the door or jump on someone.

Once your puppy is reliably sitting for you at least 50% of the time with voice command, also include the hand signal for "Sit", so that they will hear the word and also see the signal.
While you can use any hand signal, the universal hand signal for "Sit" is:

Right arm (palm open facing upward) parallel to the floor, and then raising your arm, while bent at the elbow toward your right shoulder.

Once your Teacup Yorkie is sitting reliable for you, remove the verbal "Sit" and replace it with the hand signal.

It's important to begin teaching hand signals during the adolescent stage of your puppy's life, because this will also help them to communicate in a way that is more natural for a dog — by watching you and feeling your energy, rather than always having to hear you speak a command.

As well, because the action of sitting helps to calm the mind of an excited puppy (or dog), teaching your puppy the "Sit" command is a very important part of their daily interactions with your family members as well as people you may meet when out on a walk.

When you ask your puppy to "Sit" before you interact in any way with them, before you go out or in every door, before you feed them, etc., you are helping to quiet their mind, while making it more difficult for them to jump, lunge or disappear out a door.

The adolescent stage in a young dog's life is the perfect time to begin teaching hand signals for all your common commands, because they must look at you to understand what is expected of them, and when they are looking at you, they are more focused and less likely to take matters into their own paws.

## 10. Giving Up is Not an Option

Too often we humans get frustrated and give up on our dogs when they change from being the cute, cuddly and mostly obedient little puppy they once were, and become all kinds of trouble you never bargained for, as they grow into their adolescent stage.

Often times, it will be during the confusing adolescent stage of a dog's life that they find themselves abandoned and behind bars as their humans who promised to love and protect them, leave their once loved fur friend at the local pound or SPCA.

First of all, not all dogs go through a crazy adolescent period, and secondly, even if they do, please read this section carefully humans, because you can live through puppy adolescence and come out the other side relatively unscathed and a much more knowledgeable and patient guardian.

Congratulations are in order because you've been successful with potty training your young Teacup Yorkie puppy and with teaching them to sleep in their own kennel at night.

## Chapter 16: Training

Further, you've lived through the teething troubles, the chewing and the hand nipping and you no longer have to get up at 3:00 a.m. to let your puppy out to relieve themself.

As well, you've taught your Teacup Yorkie puppy their first few basic commands, and socialized them with many other dogs, people and places, so you should feel proud of all your accomplishments and the leaps and bounds you and your puppy have accomplished together over the last several months.

Even though your adolescent puppy may be starting to act like a Tasmanian devil, and you may be having second thoughts, now is not the time to give up on them and yourself just because it may seem like someone switched your dog when you weren't looking.

Now is the time to remain calmly consistent and persistent, and to know that you will eventually be able to enjoy the happy rewards of all those months of diligent puppy training.

Yes, it can be quite a shock when what used to be your well behaved little darling who never chewed anything they weren't supposed to suddenly get it into their head to eat all the tassels off your Persian rug or chew through a seat belt in your vehicle during the short 15 minutes you were shopping.

Even more disconcerting might be when your previously obedient and loving Teacup Yorkie puppy, who always listened to your directions, suddenly appears to have gone deaf and can't remember their name when you call them to follow you inside the house, and instead they take off running after a cat three blocks away.

And then, what happened to that quiet little puppy that never appeared to have a mean bone in their body that now spends most of their time at the window barking and growling at everything and everyone passing by?

her digestive system may no longer be functioning at peak performance.

Therefore, feeding a high quality, protein-based food will be important for a senior dog's continued health.

As well, if your older Teacup Yorkie is overweight, you will want to help them shed excess pounds so that they will not be placing undue stress on their joints or heart.

The best way to accomplish this is by feeding smaller quantities of a higher quality food.

**e) Clean and Parasite Free**

The last thing an aging Teacup Yorkie should have to deal with is the misery of itching and scratching, so make sure that you continue to give them regular baths with the appropriate shampoos and conditioners to keep their coat and skin comfortable and free from biting bugs.

**f) Plenty of Water**

Proper hydration is essential for helping to keep an older Teacup Yorkie comfortable.

Water is life giving for every creature, so make certain that your aging dog has easy access to plenty of clean, fresh water which will help to improve their energy and digestion and also prevent dehydration which can add to joint stiffness.

**g) Keep Them Warm**

Just as older humans feel the cold more, so do older dogs. Keeping your senior Teacup Yorkie warm will help to alleviate some of the pain of their joint stiffness or arthritis. Make sure their bed or kennel is not kept in a drafty location and perhaps consider a heated bed for them.

## Chapter 18: Caring for Aging Dogs

Being aware that an aging Teacup Yorkie will be experiencing many symptoms that are similar to an aging human will help you to understand how best to keep them safe and as comfortable as possible during this golden time in their lives.

## 2. How to Make Them Comfortable

### a) Regular Checkups

During this time in your Teacup Yorkie's life, when their immune systems become weakened and they may be experiencing pain, you will want to get into the habit of taking your senior Teacup Yorkie for regular veterinarian checkups. Take them for a checkup every six months so that early detection of any problems can quickly be attended to and solutions for helping to keep your aging Teacup Yorkie comfortable can be provided.

### b) No Rough Play

An older Teacup Yorkie will not have the same energy or willingness to play that they did when they were younger, therefore, do not allow younger children to rough house with an older dog. Explain to them that the dog is getting older and that as a result they must learn to be gentle and to leave the dog alone when it may want to rest or sleep.

### c) Mild Exercise

Dogs still love going for walks, even when they are getting older and slowing down. Although an older Teacup Yorkie will generally have less energy, they still need to exercise and keep moving, and taking them out regularly for shorter or slower walks will keep them healthier and happier long into old age.

### d) Best Quality Food

Everyone has heard the saying, *"you are what you eat"* and for a senior dog, what he or she eats is even more important as his or

## Chapter 18: Caring for Aging Dogs

Dogs that have lost both their hearing and their sight will need to be close to you so that they can relax and not feel nervous, and so that you can communicate by touching parts of their body.

Generally speaking, even when a dog becomes blind and/or deaf, their powerful sense of smell is still functioning, which means that they will be able to smell where you are and navigate their environment by using their nose.

**d) More Bathroom Breaks**

Bathroom breaks may need to become more frequent in older dogs who may lose their ability to hold it for longer periods of time, so be prepared to be more watchful and to offer them opportunities to go outside more frequently during the day.

You may also want to place a pee pad near the door, in case they just can't hold it long enough, or if you have not already taught them to bathroom on an indoor potty patch, or pee pad, now may be the time for this alternative bathroom arrangement.

A dog who has been house trained for years will feel the shame and upset of not being able to hold it long enough to get to their regular bathroom location, so be kind and do whatever you need to do in order to help them not to have to feel bad about failing bowel or bladder control.

Our beloved canine companions may also begin to show signs of cognitive decline and changes in the way their brain functions, similar to what happens to humans suffering from Alzheimer's, where they start to wander about aimlessly, sometimes during the middle of the night.

Make sure that if this is happening with your senior Teacup Yorkie at nighttime, that they cannot accidentally fall down stairs or harm themselves in any way.

## Chapter 18: Caring for Aging Dogs

Just as research and science has improved our human quality of life in our senior years, the same is becoming true for our canine counterparts who are able to benefit from dietary supplements and pharmaceutical products to help them be as comfortable as possible in their senior years.

Of course, there will be some inconveniences associated with keeping a dog with advancing years around the home, however, your Teacup Yorkie deserves no less than to spend their final days in your loving care after they have unconditionally given you their entire lives.

**c) Geriatric Dogs**

Being aware of the changes that are likely occurring in a senior dog will help you to better care for them during their geriatric years.

For instance, most dogs will experience hearing loss and visual impairment, and how you help them will depend upon which goes first (hearing or sight).

For instance, if a dog's hearing is compromised, then using more hand signals will be helpful.

Deaf dogs will still be able to hear louder noises and feel vibrations, therefore hand clapping, knocking on walls, doors or furniture, using a loud clicker or stomping your foot on the floor may be a way to get their attention.

If a senior dog loses their eyesight, most dogs will still be able to easily navigate their familiar surroundings, and you will only need to be extra watchful on their behalf when taking them to unfamiliar territory.

If they still have their hearing, you will be able to assist your dog with verbal cues and commands.

# Chapter 18: Caring for Aging Dogs

## 1. What to Be Aware Of

As a result of many modern advances in veterinarian care, improvements in diet and nutrition and general knowledge concerning proper care of our canine companions, our dogs are able to enjoy longer, healthier lives.

As such, when caring for our canine companions, we need to be aware of behavioral and physical changes that will affect our dogs as they approach old age.

While each dog's individual health, genetics, and spirit will affect how old they seem, and they may remain quite as they get older active, a Teacup Yorkie will be entering their senior years at around 8 to 10 years of age.

**a) Physiological Changes**

As our beloved canine companions enter into their senior years, they may be suffering from very similar, physical aging problems that affect us humans, such as pain, stiffness and arthritis, and inability to control their bowels and bladder.

Any of these problems will reduce a dog's willingness to want to exercise.

**b) Behavioral Changes**

Further, a senior Teacup Yorkie may experience behavioral changes resulting from loss of hearing and sight, such as disorientation, fear or startle reactions and overall grumpiness from any number of physical problems that could be causing them pain whenever they move.

## 6. Animal Poison Control Centre

The ASPCA Animal Poison Control Center is staffed 24 hours a day, 365 days a year and is a valuable resource for learning about what plants are toxic and possibly poisonous to your dog.

**a) USA Poison Emergency**

Call: 1 (888) 426-4435

When calling the Poison Emergency number, your credit card may be charged with a $65. ((£39.42) consultation fee.

**b) UK Poison Emergency**

Call: 0800-213-6680 - Pet Poison Helpline (payable service)

Call: 0300 1234 999 - RSPCA

www.aspca.org = ASPCA Poison Control.

If you keep toxic cleaning substances (including fertilizers, vermin or snail poisons and vehicle products) in your home, garage or garden shed, always keep them behind closed doors.

As well, keep any medications where your Teacup Yorkie can never get to them, and seriously consider eliminating the use of any and all toxic products, for the health of both yourself, your family and your best fur friends.

## 4. Garden Plants

Please note that there are also many outdoor plants that can be toxic or poisonous to your puppy or dog, therefore, always check what plants are growing in your garden and if any may be harmful, remove them or make certain that your Teacup Yorkie puppy or adult dog cannot eat them.

Cornell University, Department of Animal Science lists many different categories of poisonous plants affecting dogs, including house plants, flower garden plants, vegetable garden plants, plants found in swamps or moist areas, plants found in fields, trees and shrubs, plants found in wooded areas, and ornamental plants.

## 5. Why Does My Dog Eat Grass?

Also, be aware that many puppies and adult dogs will eat grass, just because. Perhaps they are curious, bored, or need a little fiber in their diet.

Remember that canines are natural scavengers always on the look out for something they can eat, and so long as the grass is healthy and has not been sprayed with toxic chemicals, a little grass eating should not be a concern.

**Satin Pothos**: (silk pothos), if eaten by a dog, the plant may cause irritation to the dog's mouth, lips and tongue, while the dog may also experience vomiting, difficulty swallowing and drooling.

The plants noted above are only a few of the more common household plants, and every conscientious Dog guardian will want to educate themselves before bringing plants into the home that could be toxic to their canine companions.

## 3. Poison Proof Your Home

You can learn about many potentially toxic and poisonous sources both inside and outside your home by visiting the ASPCA Animal Poison Control Center website.

Always keep your veterinarian's emergency number in a place where you can quickly access it, as well as the Emergency Poison Control telephone number, in case you suspect that your dog may have been poisoned.

Knowing what to do if you suspect your dog may have been poisoned and being able to quickly contact the right people could save your dog's life.

*Chapter 17: Poisonous Foods & Plants*

**Jade Plant**: has many other names, including "baby jade, Chinese rubber plant, dwarf rubber plant, friendship tree, jade tree, or Japanese rubber plant". While exactly what is toxic to dogs in this plant is unknown, a dog eating a Jade plant can suffer from loss of coordination and depression as well as a slowed heart rate.

**Lilies**: some plants of the lily family can be toxic to dogs. The peace lily (also known as Mauna Loa) is known to be toxic to dogs. Eating the peace lily or calla lily can cause vomiting, irritation to the dog's tongue and lips, problems swallowing and increased drooling.

*Chapter 17: Poisonous Foods & Plants*

**Elephant Ear**: also known as *"cape, caladium, malanga, pai, taro and via sori,"* contains a chemical which is similar to a chemical also found in dieffenbachia. A dog's toxic reaction to elephant ear is similar, including oral irritation, problems swallowing, increased drooling, and vomiting.

**Heartleaf Philodendron**: also known as *"cordatum, split-leaf philodendron, fiddle leaf, fruit salad plant, horsehead philodendron, panda plant, red emerald, red princess, and saddle leaf"*, is a very common, easy-to-grow houseplant that contains a chemical irritating to the mouth, tongue and lips of dogs. An affected dog may also experience difficulty swallowing, vomiting and increased drooling.

*Chapter 17: Poisonous Foods & Plants*

**Cyclamen**: also known as *"Sowbread"*, is a pretty, flowering plant that, if eaten, can cause diarrhea, vomiting and increased salivation. If a dog eats a large amount of the plant's tubers, usually found underneath the soil at the root level, heart rhythm problems can occur, which may result in seizures or even death.

**Dieffenbachia**: also known as *"exotica, dumb cane and tropic snow"* contains a chemical that is a poisonous deterrent to animals. If a dog eats the plant, they will experience mouth irritation, especially on the tongue and lips that can lead to increased drooling, problems swallowing and vomiting.

may cause vomiting and/or reddish urine.

**Asparagus Fern**: is also known as *"lace fern, emerald fern, emerald feather, sprengeri fern and plumosa fern"*. The toxic agent in this plant is sapogenin, which is a steroid found in a variety of plants. Repeated exposure to the berries of this plant cause vomiting, diarrhea and/or abdominal pain or skin inflammation.

**Corn Plant**: also known as *"ribbon plant, cornstalk plant, dragon tree and dracaena"*, is toxic to dogs. Saponin is the offensive chemical compound found in this plant. If the plant is eaten, vomiting (with or without blood), loss of appetite, depression and/or increased drooling can occur.

or products far away from your beloved Teacup Yorkie and you'll help them to live a long and healthy life.

## 2. Poisonous Household Plants

Many common house plants are actually poisonous to our canine companions, and although many dogs simply will ignore house plants, some will attempt to eat anything, especially puppies who want to taste everything in their new world.

More than 700 plant species contain toxins that may harm or be fatal to puppies or dogs, depending on the size of the puppy or dog and how much they may eat.

Therefore, it is especially important to be aware of household plants that could be toxic when you are sharing your home with a new puppy.

Following is a short list of the more common household plants, what they look like, the different names they are known by, and what symptoms might be apparent if your puppy or dog decides to eat them.

**Aloe Plant**: also known as *"medicine plant or Barbados aloe"*, is a very common succulent plant that is toxic to dogs. The toxic agent in this plant is Aloin.

This bitter yellow substance is found in most aloe species and

## Chapter 17: Poisonous Foods & Plants

If you suspect your dog has eaten cigarette butts, seek immediate veterinary help.

**TIP**: when your dog is a very young puppy, use a double leash, collar and harness arrangement, so that you can still teach them to walk on leash with a Martingale collar around their neck, but can also attach the second leash to their harness so that you can easily lift them over enticing cigarette butts or other toxic garbage they may be trying to eat during your walks.

**Tomatoes**: tomatoes contain a substance called atropine, which can cause tremors, dilated pupils and an irregular heartbeat in a puppy or dog that eats them. The greatest amount of atropine will be found in the stalks and leaves of the tomato plant, next is the green tomato (before it ripens), and then ripe tomatoes.

**Xylitol**: is an artificial sweetener often found in many candies, gums, breath mints, toothpastes and mouthwashes that is recognized by the National Animal Poison Control Center to be a poison risk to dogs.

When puppies or dogs eat products containing Xylitol, it causes a sudden release of insulin, which in turn causes low blood sugar, which can also cause liver damage.

Within 30 minutes after eating a product containing Xylitol, the dog may vomit, be lethargic (tired), and/or be uncoordinated. However, some signs of toxicity can also be delayed for hours or even for a few days. Xylitol toxicity in dogs can be fatal if left untreated.

Please be aware that the above list is just some of the more common foods that can be toxic or fatal to our fur friends and that there are many other foods we should never be feeding our dogs.

If you have one of those dogs who will happily eat anything that looks or smells even slightly like food, or even if not food, but is enticing for a puppy or dog to eat, be certain to keep these foods

## Chapter 17: Poisonous Foods & Plants

drooling, voiding of urine and feces, vomiting, muscle spasm, staggering, and coma before death.

Dogs suffering from cyanide poisoning that live more than 2 hours after onset of symptoms will usually recover.

**Raw Salmon or Trout**: Salmon Poisoning Disease (SPD) can be a problem for anyone who goes fishing with their dog, or feeds their dog a raw meat diet that includes raw salmon or trout.

When a snail is infected and then is eaten by the fish as part of the food chain, the dog is exposed when it eats the infected fish.

A sudden onset of symptoms can occur 5-7 days after eating the infected fish. In the acute stages, gastrointestinal symptoms are quite similar to canine parvovirus.

SPD has a mortality rate of up to 90%, can be diagnosed with a fecal sample and is treatable if caught in time.

Prevention is simple, cook all fish before feeding it to your Teacup Yorkie and immediately see your veterinarian if you suspect that your dog has eaten raw salmon or trout.

**Tobacco**: all forms of tobacco, including patches, nicotine gum and chewing tobacco can be fatal to dogs if eaten.

Signs of poisoning can appear quite rapidly (within an hour or less) and may include diarrhea, vomiting, a heightened state of activity, excessive drooling and panting.

Depending upon how much a dog may have eaten, more acute signs of poisoning may cause twitching, leading to collapse and coma due to heart attack that will cause death.

Never leave tobacco products within reach of your puppy or dog, and be careful not to let them pick up discarded cigarette butts when they are young puppies.

## Chapter 17: Poisonous Foods & Plants

**Macadamia Nuts**: are commonly found in candies and chocolates. Although the mechanism of macadamia nut toxicity is not well understood, the clinical signs in dogs having eaten these nuts include depression, weakness, vomiting, tremors, joint pain, and pale gums.

Signs can occur within 12 hours after eating. In some cases, symptoms can resolve themselves without treatment within 24 to 48 hours. However, keeping a close eye on your Teacup Yorkie will be strongly recommended.

**Mushrooms**: mushroom poisoning can be fatal if certain species of mushrooms are eaten.

The most commonly reported severely toxic species of mushroom in the US is Amanita phalloides (Death Cap mushroom), which is also quite a common species found in most parts of Britain. Other Amanita species are also toxic.

This deadly mushroom is often found growing in grassy or wooded areas near various deciduous and coniferous trees, which mean that if you're out walking with your dog in the woods, they could easily find these mushrooms.

Eating them can cause severe liver disease and neurological disorders. If you suspect your dog has eaten these mushrooms, immediately take them to your veterinarian, as the recommended treatment is to induce vomiting and to give activated charcoal. Further treatment for liver disease may also be necessary.

**Pits and Seeds**: many seeds and pits found in a variety of fruits, including apples, apricots, cherries, pears and plums, contain cyanogenic glycosides that can cause cyanide poisoning in your dog.

The symptoms of cyanide poisoning usually occur within 15-20 minutes to a few hours after eating and symptoms can include initial excitement, followed by rapid respiration rate, salivation or

## Chapter 17: Poisonous Foods & Plants

create a rupture or puncture of the stomach lining or intestinal tract.

Especially dangerous are cooked turkey and chicken legs, ham, pork chop and veal bones. Symptoms of choking include:

- Pale or blue gums
- Gasping breathing or panting
- Pawing or scratching at the face
- Slowed, shallow breathing
- Collapse and unconsciousness with dilated pupils

**Grapes and Raisins**: can cause acute (sudden) kidney failure in dogs. While it is not known what the toxic agent is in this fruit, clinical signs can occur within 24 hours of eating and include vomiting, diarrhea, and lethargy (tiredness).

Other signs of illness caused from eating grapes or raisins relate to the eventual shutdown of kidney functioning.

**Garlic and Onions**: contain chemicals that damage red blood cells by rupturing them so that they lose their ability to carry oxygen effectively, which leave the dog short of oxygen, causing what is called *"hemolytic anemia"*.

Poisoning can occur when a dog eats a large amount of garlic or onions all at once, or when eating repeated meals containing smaller amounts.

Cooking does not reduce the potential toxicity of onions and garlic.

**NOTE**: fresh, cooked, and/or powdered garlic or onions are commonly found in baby food, which is sometimes given to dogs when they are sick, therefore, be certain to carefully read food labels before feeding to your Teacup Yorkie.

## Chapter 17: Poisonous Foods & Plants

types of chocolate contain different amounts of theobromine and caffeine.

For example, dark chocolate and baking chocolate or cocoa powder contain more of these compounds than milk chocolate does, therefore, a dog would need to eat more milk chocolate in order to become ill.

However, even a few ounces of chocolate can be enough to cause illness or death in a puppy or smaller dog, therefore, no amount or type of chocolate should be considered safe for a dog to eat.

A dog suffering from having eaten chocolate may display symptoms that include diarrhea, vomiting, increased heart rate, restless behavior, muscle tremors, or seizures. If they have eaten enough of it, they could die within 24 hours of eating.

During many holidays such as Christmas, New Year's, Valentine's, Easter and Halloween, chocolate is often more easily accessible to curious dogs, especially from children who are not so careful with where they might keep their Halloween or Easter egg stash and who are an easy mark for a hungry dog.

In some cases, people unwittingly poison their dogs by offering them chocolate as a treat or leaving chocolate cookies or frosted cake easily within licking distance.

**Caffeine**: beverages containing caffeine, such as soda, tea, coffee, and chocolate, act as a stimulant and can accelerate your dog's heartbeat to a dangerous level. Dogs eating caffeine have been known to have seizures, some of which are fatal.

**Cooked Bones**: can be extremely hazardous for a dog because the bones become brittle when cooked which causes them to splinter when the dog chews on them.

The splinters have sharp edges that have been known to become stuck in the teeth, and cause choking when caught in the throat or

# Chapter 17: Poisonous Foods & Plants

## 1. Poisonous Foods

While some dogs are smart enough not to want to eat foods that can harm or kill them, there are those canine companions that will eat absolutely anything they can get their teeth on, whether or not it's food.

As conscientious guardians for our fur friends, it will always be our responsibility to make certain that when we share our homes with a dog, we never leave foods (or other products) that could be toxic or lethal to them easily within their reach.

While there are many foods that can be toxic to a dog, the following alphabetical list contains some of the more common foods that can seriously harm or even kill our dogs including:

**Bread Dough**: if your dog eats bread dough, their body heat will cause the dough to rise inside the stomach. As the dough expands during the rising process, alcohol is produced.

Dogs who have eaten bread dough may experience stomach bloating, abdominal pain, vomiting, disorientation and depression. Because bread dough can rise to many times its original size, eating only a small amount will cause a problem for any dog.

**Broccoli**: the toxic ingredient in broccoli is isothiocynate. While it may cause stomach upset, it probably won't be very harmful unless the amount eaten is more than 10% of the dog's total daily diet.

**Chocolate**: contains theobromine, a chemical that is toxic to dogs in large enough quantities. Chocolate also contains caffeine, which is found in coffee, tea, and certain soft drinks. Different

## 16. Overheating

Be very careful, when training or walking your Teacup Yorkie outside during hot weather, so that you do not allow them to become overheated.

When it's warm outside, always carry water with you to help keep them hydrated.

**TIP**: if your Teacup Yorkie has a coat that is darker colored, you can easily help to keep them cooler on hot, sunny days by having them wear a light weight vest that is a lighter color than their own coat.

Remember that smaller dogs are close to heated pavement or road surfaces, which means that on a hot, sunny day, they will literally be heated from both the bottom and the top.

If the pavement or other walking surface is very hot, do not allow them to walk on it. Instead, take them to a grassy area for their exercise.

## 15. Behavioral Issues

It can be difficult, if not impossible to generalize or speculate with respect to alleviating possible behavioral issues or problems you may encounter with your dog because, in most cases, a dog suffering from behavioral issues requires the assistance of a dog whisperer or dog psychologist.

When reading anything about how to prevent or cure behavioral issues, please be aware that behavioral problems most often cannot be properly assessed or cured by reading a book.

The reason for this is because there are just too many variables and unique situations, individual dogs, individual humans, unique circumstances, and endless reasons why they may have developed any particular behavioral issue.

Therefore, without knowing the dog's particulars and all the history of what has transpired between the Teacup Yorkie and their guardian that came before or how the problem might have manifested itself, attempting to write about how to cure a particular issue will be no more than a best guess.

This is why someone whose dog is suffering from a specific behavioral issue that is in turn, at the least embarrassing, or at the worst dangerous, and driving the humans and the entire neighborhood crazy, must be properly addressed by engaging the services of a competent, professional dog whisperer (psychologist or behaviorist) who can ask many questions, properly assess the situation and then design a unique plan for alleviating the problem.

Believe it or not, there are far more problems created with smaller companion dogs than larger dogs, and this is usually a direct result of the human guardian not treating their small companion like a dog, with the subsequent rules and boundaries that go along with being an obedient and happy family member.

## Chapter 16: Training

ensure a happy and healthy companion, make sure that you get them involved in as much activity as possible, including advanced training or canine sports.

When your Teacup Yorkie is a full grown adult (approximately two years of age), you will definitely want to begin more complicated or advanced training sessions.

They will enjoy it and when you have the desire and patience, there is no end to the commands, tricks, routines or canine sports you can teach a willing Teacup Yorkie.

For instance, you may wish to teach your adult Teacup Yorkie more advanced tricks, such as how to dance, or the opposite sided paw shakes or roll overs, which are more difficult than you might expect.

If you and your Teacup Yorkie are really enjoying learning new tricks together, you might want to advance to teaching them the hand signals for *"commando crawl"*, how to *"speak"* or to *"jump through the human hoop"*, or perhaps get them involved in a fun sport.

All of these tricks and many more are fun to teach and will exercise both your Teacup Yorkie's mind and body by taking advantage of their natural ability to excel as an entertaining circus performer.

As well, the more control you have over your Teacup Yorkie, the easier it will be to teach them a fun sport, such as Agility or Freestyle dance.

The only restriction to how far you can go with training your adult Teacup Yorkie will be your imagination and their personal ability or desire to perform, which with the exuberant Teacup Yorkie will be endless.

## Chapter 16: Training

Find a quiet space with few distractions and sit or stand in front of your dog and ask them to "Sit".

Have a treat nearby (on a countertop or table) and when they sit, use both of your hands to lift up their front paws into the sitting pretty position, while saying the command *"Sit Pretty"*. Help them balance in this position while you praise them and give them the treat.

Once your Teacup Yorkie can do the balancing part of the trick quite easily without your help, sit or stand in front of your dog while asking them to *"Sit Pretty"* and hold the treat above their head, at the level their nose would be when they sit pretty.

**TIP**: when first beginning this trick, place your Teacup Yorkie beside a wall so they can use the wall to help them balance.

If they attempt to stand on their back legs to get the treat, you may be holding the treat too high, which will encourage them to stand on their back legs to reach it. Go back to the first step and put them back into the *"Sit"* position and again lift their paws while their backside remains on the floor.

**Sit Pretty**: hold your straight arm, fully extended, over your dog's head with a closed fist.

Make this a fun and entertaining time for your Teacup Yorkie and practice a few times every day until they can *"Sit Pretty"* on hand signal command every time you ask. A young Teacup Yorkie puppy should be able to easily learn these basic tricks before they are six months old and when you are patient and make your training sessions short and fun for your dog, they will be eager to learn more.

## 14. Adult Training

The Teacup Yorkie is a highly intelligent, athletic breed that will be skillful in many different dog sports, therefore, in order to

Practice every day until they are 100% reliable with this trick, and then it will be time to add another trick to their repertoire.

## b) Roll Over

You will find that just like your Teacup Yorkie is naturally either right or left pawed, that they will also naturally want to roll either to the right or the left side. Take advantage of this by asking your dog to roll to the side they naturally prefer.

Sit with your dog on the floor and put them in a lie down position. Hold a treat in your hand and place it close to their nose without allowing them to grab it, and while they are in the lying position, move the treat to the right or left side of their head so that they have to roll over to get to it.

You will very quickly see which side they want to naturally roll to, and once you see this, move the treat to this side. When they roll over to this side, immediately give them the treat and praise them.

You can say the verbal cue *"Over"* while you demonstrate the hand signal motion (moving your right hand in a circular motion) or moving the treat from one side of their head to the other with a half circle motion.

**Roll Over**: moving your right or left arm/hand in a small half circular motion, in the direction you wish your dog to roll toward.

Once your Teacup Yorkie can roll over every time you ask, it will be time to teach them another trick.

## c) Sit Pretty

While this trick is a little more complicated, and most dogs pick up on it very quickly, remember that every dog is different so always exercise patience.

for a job well done.

## 13. Simple Tricks

When teaching your Teacup Yorkie tricks, in order to give them extra incentive, find a treat that they really like, and give the treat as a reward and to help solidify a good performance.

Most dogs will be extra attentive during training sessions when they know that they will be rewarded with their favorite treats.

If your Teacup Yorkie is less than six months old when you begin teaching them tricks, keep your training sessions short (no more than 5 or 10 minutes) and fun, and as they become adults, you can extend your sessions as they will be able to maintain their focus for longer periods of time.

**a) Shake a Paw**

Who doesn't love a dog that knows how to shake a paw? This is one of the easiest tricks to teach your Teacup Yorkie.

**TIP**: most dogs are naturally either right or left pawed. If you know which paw your dog favors, ask them to shake this paw.

Find a quiet place to practice, without noisy distractions or other pets, and stand or sit in front of your dog. Place them in the sitting position and have a treat in your left hand.

Say the command *"Shake"* while putting your right hand behind their left or right paw and pulling the paw gently toward yourself until you are holding their paw in your hand. Immediately praise them and give them the treat.

Most dogs will learn the "Shake" trick quite quickly, and very soon, once you put out your hand, your Teacup Yorkie will immediately lift their paw and put it into your hand, without your assistance or any verbal cue.

Slowly remove the treat as reward and replace the treat with a "life reward", such as a chest rub or a scratch behind the ears and your happy smile.

If your Teacup Yorkie is not particularly treat motivated, lift up and slightly back on the leash when asking them to sit (stand in front of them), and if they still are having difficulties, reach down with your free hand, place it across your dog's back at the place where the back legs join the hip and gently squeeze.

Remember -- Do NOT simply push down on your dog's back to force their hind legs to collapse under them as this pressure could harm their spine or leg joints.

**c) Stay**

**Stay**: right armed fully extended toward your dog's head, palm open, hand bent up at the wrist.

Once your Teacup Yorkie is in the "Sit" position, ask them to "Stay" with both the verbal cue and the hand signal.

**TIP**: if you are right-handed use your right arm and hand for the signal, and if you are left-handed, use your left arm and hand for the signal. Using your dominant hand will be much more effective because your strongest energy emanates from the palm of your dominant hand.

While your dog is sitting and staying, slowly back away from them. If they move from their position, calmly put them back into Sit and ask them to "Stay" again, using both the verbal cue and the hand signal.

Continue to practice this until your dog understands that you want them to stay sitting and not move toward you.

With all commands, when your Teacup Yorkie is just learning, be patient and always reward them with a treat and your happy praise

## Chapter 16: Training

When first teaching hand signals to your Teacup Yorkie, always show the hand signal for the command at the same time you say the word.

If they are totally ignoring the command, it will be time to incorporate a light lunge line, which is a very long leash to help you teach the "Come" command.

Simply attach a 20-foot line to their collar and let them sniff about in a large yard or at your neighborhood park.

At your leisure, firmly ask them to "Come" and show the hand signal. If they do not immediately come to you, give a firm tug with the lunge line, so that they understand what you are asking of them.

If they still do not "Come" toward you, simply reel them in until they are in front of you. Then let them wander about again, until you are ready to ask them to "Come".

Repeat this process until your Teacup Yorkie responds correctly at least 80% of the time. You can also reinforce the command by giving a treat when they come back to you when asked. Always ask them to "Sit" when they return to you.

**b) Sit**

**Sit**: right arm (palm open facing upward) parallel to the floor, and then raise your arm, while bent at the elbow toward your shoulder.

Sit is a very simple, yet extremely valuable command for all puppies and dogs.

If your dog is not sitting on command, try holding a treat above and slightly behind their head, so that when they look up for it they may automatically sit in order to see the treat they want.

your puppy will always enjoy correctly responding and immediately returning to you.

Practice these three basic commands everywhere you go, and use the "Sit" command every time you go for a walk, before you open the door, after you are on the other side of the door, before you go down the stairs, once you are at the bottom of the stairs, and every time you stop when you are on your walk, and pretty soon you will have a puppy who automatically sits whenever you stop moving.

As your puppy gets older, and their attention span increases, you will be able to train for longer periods of time.

## 12. Hand Signals

Hand signal training is by far the most useful and efficient training method for every dog, including the Teacup Yorkie.

This is because all too often we inundate our canine companions with a great deal of chatter and noise that they really do not understand because English is not their first language.

Contrary to what some humans might think, the first language of a Teacup Yorkie, or any dog, is a combination of sensing energy and watching body language, which requires no spoken word or sound. Therefore, when we humans take the time to teach our dog hand signals for all their basic commands, we are communicating with them at a level they instinctively understand, plus we are helping them to become a focused follower, as they must watch us to understand what is required of them.

### a) Come

**Come**: you can kneel down for this command or stay standing. Open your arms wide like you are hugging a very large tree. This hand signal can be seen from a long distance.

## b) Sit

The "Sit" and "Stay" commands are both easy commands to teach that will help to keep your Teacup Yorkie puppy safe and out of danger in most every circumstance.

Find a quiet time to teach these commands when your puppy is not overly tired.

Ask your puppy to "Sit" and if they do not yet understand the command, show them what you mean by gently squeezing with your thumb and middle finger, the area across the back that joins with their back legs.

Do not just push them down into a sit as this can cause damage to their back or joints. When they sit, give them a treat and praise them.

When you say the word "Sit", at the same time show them the hand signal for this command, which is bending your arm at the elbow and raising your right hand, palm open facing upward, toward your shoulder.

## c) Stay

Once your Teacup Yorkie puppy can reliably "Sit", say the word "Stay" and hold your outstretched arm, palm open toward their head and back away a few steps.

If they try to follow, calmly say "No" and put them back into "Sit". Give a treat and then say again, "Stay" with the hand signal and back away a few steps.

Once your puppy is sitting and staying, you can then ask them to "Come". Don't forget to use the open arms hand signal for "Come." Be a little excited with the "Come" command so that

## Chapter 16: Training

Also, introduce the hand signals that go along with the verbal commands so that once they learn both, you can remove the verbal commands in favor of just hand signals.

### a) Come

While the intelligent Teacup Yorkie puppy will be capable of learning commands and tricks at a young age, the first and most important command you need to teach your puppy is the recall, or *"Come"* command.

The hand signal for "Come" is your arms spread wide open. This is a command they can see from a great distance.

Begin the "Come" command inside your home. Go into a larger room, such as your living room area. Place your puppy in front of you and attach their leash or a longer line to their Martingale collar, while you back away from them a few feet.

Say the command "Come" in an excited, happy voice and hold your arms open wide. If they do not immediately come to you, gently give a tug on the leash so that they understand that they are supposed to move toward you. When they come to you praise them and give a treat they really enjoy.

Once your puppy can accomplish a "Come" command almost every time inside your home, you can then graduate them to a nearby park or quiet outside area where you will repeat the process. You may want to purchase an extra long, lightweight line (25 or 50 feet) so that you are always attached to your Teacup Yorkie puppy and can encourage them in the right direction should they become distracted.

## Chapter 16: Training

While it's usually hormones that are the major cause of behavioral changes in your adolescent puppy, there are also physical changes occurring at the same time that you may not be aware of.

For instance, your puppy will be going through physical growth spurts which might be causing them some pain, as well as changes related to growth in their brain while your puppy's cerebral cortex becomes more involved in thinking for itself.

Usually, during this time of brain growth, a puppy will be trying to make choices for themselves, and may or may not yet be capable of making the right choices. This is why their behavior can appear to be quite erratic.

During the early adolescent period of brain development in your Teacup Yorkie puppy, the signals sometimes get mixed up and rerouted, which can result in the perplexing responses you might notice, when for instance, you ask you puppy to sit and they stare dumbly at you, even though they learned this command months ago.

Don't worry because your previous training will return.

## 11. Re-visit Basic First Commands

All that's necessary for effectively teaching your puppy their basic first commands is a calm, consistent approach, combined with your endless patience.

Many puppies are ready to begin training at about 10 to 12 weeks of age, however, be careful not to overdo it when they are less than four to six months of age, as their attention span will be short. Make your training sessions no more than 5 or 10 minutes, positive and pleasant with lots of praise and/or treats so that your puppy will be looking forward to their next session.

## Chapter 16: Training

Welcome to the world of canine adolescence where it appears that your puppy has turned into some sort of monster and all your previous hard work was for nothing.

Of course, this dramatic switch from being the world's best puppy into the monster you can no longer control is not true for all puppies, as every puppy is unique.

However, being prepared for the worst will help you ride any impending storm and get you both out the other side where you can enjoy an even closer relationship than you previously had.

The adolescent phase may be very subtle for your Teacup Yorkie puppy or on the other hand, it may be so dramatic that you're starting to feel guilty every time you drive past the local SPCA or dog pound because thoughts of rehoming are running through your head.

If you are at the stage with your puppy that you are having great difficulties and wondering if you made the right decision to share your home with a dog, rest assured that puppy adolescence is a normal phase of their development, which can be managed, and which will definitely pass.

As well, if you are finding yourself totally overwhelmed, there are many professionals who can provide valuable assistance to help you through this stage of your puppy's development.

For most puppies, adolescence will begin between the ages of five and seven months and this is also the time that you need to be making an appointment at your veterinarian's office to have your puppy spayed or neutered.

Although neutering or spaying will not prevent undesirable adolescent behavior entirely, it can certainly reduce the intensity of it, as during this period there are hormonal changes occurring that will affect your puppy's behavior.

## Chapter 18: Caring for Aging Dogs

Be aware that your aging Teacup Yorkie will be more sensitive to extremes in temperature, and it will be up to you to make sure that they are comfortable at all times, which means not too hot and not too cold.

**h) Indoor Clothing**

We humans tend to wear warmer clothing as we get older, simply because we have more difficulty maintaining a comfortable body temperature and the same will be true of our senior Teacup Yorkie companions.

Therefore, while you most likely already have a selection of outdoor clothing appropriate to the climate in which you live, you may not have considered keeping your Teacup Yorkie warm while inside the home.

Now would be the time to consider doggy t-shirts or sweater clothing options to help keep your aging companion comfortably warm both inside and out.

**i) Steps or Stairs**

If your Teacup Yorkie is allowed to sleep on the human couch or chair, but they are having difficulties getting up there as their joints are becoming stiff and painful, consider buying or making them a set of soft, foam stairs so that they do not have to make the jump to their favorite sleeping place.

**j) Comfortable Bed**

While most dogs seem to be happy with sleeping on the floor, providing a padded, soft bed will greatly help to relieve sore spots and joint pain in older dogs.

If there is a draft in the home, generally it will be at floor level, therefore, a bed that is raised up off of the floor will be warmer for your senior Teacup Yorkie.

## k) More Love and Attention

Last, but not least, make sure that you give your senior Teacup Yorkie lots of love and attention and never leave them alone for long periods of time.

When they are not feeling their best, they will want to be with you all that much more because you are their trusted guardian whom they love beyond life itself.

## 3. What is Euthanasia?

Every veterinarian will have received special training to help provide all incurably ill, injured or aged pets that have come to the end of their natural lives with a humane and gentle death, through a process called *"euthanasia"*.

When the time comes, euthanasia, or putting a dog *"to sleep"*, will usually be a two-step process.

First, the veterinarian will inject the dog with a sedative to make them sleepy, calm and comfortable.

Second, the veterinarian will inject a special drug that will peacefully stop their heart.

These drugs work in such a way that the dog will not experience any awareness whatsoever that their life is coming to an end. What they will experience is very much like what we humans experience when falling asleep under anesthesia during a surgical procedure.

Once the second stage drug has been injected, the entire process takes about 10 to 20 seconds, at which time the veterinarian will then check to make certain that the dog's heart has stopped.

There is no suffering with this process, which is a very gentle and humane way to end a dog's suffering and allow them to peacefully pass on.

## 4. When to Help a Dog Transition

The impending loss of a beloved dog is one of the most painfully difficult and emotionally devastating experiences a canine guardian will ever have to face.

For the sake of our faithful companions, because we do not want to prolong their suffering, we humans will have to do our best to look at our dog's situation practically, rather than emotionally, so that we can make the best decision for them.

They may be suffering from extreme old age and the inability to even walk outside to relieve themselves, and thus having to deal with the indignity of regularly soiling their sleeping area, they may have been diagnosed with an incurable illness that is causing them much pain, or they may have been seriously injured.

Whatever the reason for a canine companion's suffering, it will be up to their human guardian to calmly guide the end-of-life experience so that any further discomfort and distress can be minimized.

### a) What to Do If You Are Uncertain

In circumstances where it is not entirely clear how much a dog is suffering, it will be helpful to pay close attention to your Teacup Yorkie's behavior and keep a daily log or record so that you can know for certain how much of their day is difficult and painful for them, and how much is not.

When you keep a daily log, it will be easier to decide if the dog's quality of life has become so poor that it makes better sense to offer them the gift of peacefully going to sleep.

During this time of uncertainty, it will also be very important to discuss with your veterinarian what signs of suffering may be associated with the dog's particular disease or condition, so that you know what to look for.

Often a dog may still continue to eat or drink despite being upset, having difficulty breathing, excessively panting, being disoriented or in much pain, and as their caring guardians, we will have to weigh their love of eating against how much they are really suffering in all other aspects of their life.

Obviously, if a canine guardian can clearly see that their beloved companion is suffering throughout their days and nights, it will make sense to help humanely end their suffering by planning a euthanasia procedure.

We humans are often tempted to delay the inevitable moment of euthanasia, because we love our dogs so much and cannot bear the anticipation of the intense grief we know will overwhelm us when we must say our final goodbyes to our beloved fur friend.

Unfortunately, we may regret that we allowed our dog to suffer too long, and could find ourselves wishing that if only we humans had the same option, to peacefully let go, when we find ourselves in such a stage in our own lives.

## 5. Grieving a Lost Pet

Some humans do not fully recognize the terrible grief involved in losing a beloved canine friend.

There will be many who do not understand the close bond we humans can have with our dogs, which is often unlike any we have with our human counterparts.

Your friends may give you pitying looks and try to cheer you up, but if they have never experienced such a loss themselves, they may also secretly think that you are making too much fuss over "just a dog".

For some of us humans, the loss of a beloved dog is so painful that we decide never to share our lives with another, because we cannot bear the thought of going through the pain of loss again.

Expect to feel terribly sad, tearful and yes, depressed because those who are close to their canine companions will feel their loss no less acutely than the loss of a human friend or life partner.

The grieving process can take some time to recover from, and some of us never totally recover.

After the loss of a family dog, first you need to take care of yourself by making certain that you keep eating and getting regular sleep, even though you will feel an almost eerie sense of loneliness.

Losing a beloved dog is a shock to the system, which can also affect your concentration and your ability to find joy or want to participate in other activities that may be part of your daily life.

During this early grieving time you will need to take extra care while driving or performing tasks that require your concentration as you may find yourself distracted.

If there are other dogs or pets in the home, they will also be grieving the loss of a companion, and may display this by acting depressed, being off their food or showing little interest in play or games. Therefore, you need to help guide your other pets through this grieving process by keeping them busy and interested, taking them for extra walks and spending more time with them.

Many people do not wait long enough before attempting to replace a lost pet and will immediately go to the local shelter and rescue a deserving dog.

While this may help to distract you from your grieving process, this is not really fair to the new fur member of your family.

Bringing a new pet into a home that is depressed and grieving the loss of a long time canine member may create behavioral problems for the new dog who will be faced with learning all about their new home while also dealing with the unstable, sad energy of the grieving family.

A better scenario would be to allow yourself the time to properly grieve by waiting a minimum of one month to allow yourself and your family to feel happier and more stable before deciding upon sharing your home with another dog.

The grieving process will be different for everyone and you will know when the time is right to consider sharing your home with another canine companion.

## 6. The Rainbow Bridge Poem

"Just this side of heaven is a
place called Rainbow Bridge.

When an animal dies that has been
especially close to someone here,
that pet goes to Rainbow Bridge.
There are meadows and hills for all of our special friends
so they can run and play together.
There is plenty of food, water and sunshine,
and our friends are warm and comfortable.

All the animals who had been ill and old
are restored to health and vigor;
those who were hurt or maimed
are made whole and strong again,
just as we remember them in our dreams
of days and times gone by.

The animals are happy and content,
except for one small thing;
they each miss someone very special to them,
who had to be left behind.

They all run and play together,
but the day comes when one suddenly stops
and looks into the distance.
His bright eyes are intent; His eager body quivers.
Suddenly he begins to run from the group,
flying over the green grass,
his legs carrying him faster and faster.

You have been spotted,
and when you and your special friend finally meet,
you cling together in joyous reunion,
never to be parted again.
The happy kisses rain upon your face;
your hands again caress the beloved head,
 and you look once more into the trusting eyes
of your pet, so long gone from your life
but never absent from your heart.

Then you cross Rainbow Bridge together...."

- Author unknown

## 7. Memorials

There are as many ways to honor the passing of a beloved pet, as each of our fur friends is uniquely special to us.

For instance, you and your family may wish to have your companion cremated and preserve their ashes in a special urn or sprinkle their ashes along their favorite walk, or across the lake where they loved to swim.

*Chapter 18: Caring for Aging Dogs*

Perhaps you will want to have a special marker, photo bereavement, photo engraved Rainbow Bridge Poem, or wooden plaque created in honor of your lost friend.

You may wish to keep their memory close to you at all times by having a DNA remembrance pendant or bracelet designed.

As well, there are support groups, such as Rainbow Bridge, which is a grief support community, to help you and your family through this painful period of loss and grief.

# Chapter 19: Rescue Organizations

When you are considering rescuing a specific breed of dog or puppy, the first place to start your search will be with your local breeders, shelters and rescue groups.

There are many rescue site dedicated solely to the Yorkshire Terrier breed, including:

Rescue Me Yorkie Rescue
United Yorkie Rescue
Yorkie Rescue of America
Yorkshire Terrier National Rescue

## 1. Shelters

Here you can expect to pay an adoption fee to cover the cost of spaying or neutering, but this will be only a small percentage of what you would pay a breeder, and you will be saving a life at the same time.

## 2. Online Resources

Sites such as Petango, Adopt A Pet and Pet Finder can be good places to begin your search.

Each of these online resources is a central gathering site for hundreds and hundreds of local shelters, humane societies and rescue groups.

## 3. Canine Clubs and Breeders

Another place to search will be hybrid clubs or breeders in your local area. These groups may have rescue dogs available.

## Chapter 20: Resources & References

The following resources and references are listed alphabetically within their specific category and include web addresses.

### 1. Poison Control

ASPCA Poison Control [aspca.org]
Poisonous Plants Affecting Dogs - Cornell University, Department of Animal Science [ansi.cornell.edu/plants/dogs/]

### 2. Breeders, Registries & Rescues

Adopt A Pet [adoptapet.com]
Breeders Club [breedersclub.net/html/breeds/Teacup Yorkie.htm]
California Yorkie Breeders [Yorkie.californiapuppiesforsale.com]
Champ Dogs [champdogs.co.uk]
National Dog Tattoo Register [dog-register.co.uk]
National Dog Registry [nationaldogregistry.com]
North Carolina Yorkies [yorkiepuppies.webs.com]
Petango [petango.com]
Pet Finder [petfinder.com]
Rescue Me Yorkie Rescue [yorkierescueme.com]
The Kennel Club [thekennelclub.org.uk]
United Yorkie Rescue [unitedyorkierescue.org]
Yorkie Rescue of America [yorkierescueofamerica.org]
Yorkies UK [yorkiesuk.com]
Yorkshire Terrier National Rescue [yorkierescue.com]

### 3. Equipment, Supplies & Services

Andis Dog Clippers [andis.com]
CedarCide [cedarcide.com]
Dog Bowl for Your Dog [dogbowlforyourdog.com]

*Chapter 20: Resources & References*

Dremel™ Nail Grinder for Dogs
K-9 Super Heroes Dog Whispering [k-9superheroesdogwhispering.com]
Modern Puppies [modernpuppies.com]
Oster Dog Clippers [osterpro.com]
Poochie Bells™ [poochie-pets.net]
Remove Urine Odors [removeurineodors.com]
Sleepy Pod [sleepypod.com]
Tell Bell™ [tellbell.com]
Tick Twister [ticktwister.com]
ThunderShirt [thundershirt.com]
Wahl Dog Clippers [wahl.com]

## 4. Memorials

Rainbow Bridge [rainbowbridge.com]

## Published by IMB Publishing 2014

**Copyright and Trademarks**: This publication is Copyrighted 2014 by IMB Publishing. All products, publications, software and services mentioned and recommended in this publication are protected by trademarks. In such instance, all trademarks & copyright belong to the respective owners. All rights reserved. No part of this book may be reproduced or transferred in any form or by any means, graphic, electronic, or mechanical, including photocopying, recording, taping, or by any information storage retrieval system, without the written permission of the authors. Pictures used in this book are either royalty free pictures bought from stock-photo websites or have the source mentioned underneath the picture.

**Disclaimer and Legal Notice**: This product is not legal or medical advice and should not be interpreted in that manner. You need to do your own due-diligence to determine if the content of this product is right for you. The authors and the affiliates of this product are not liable for any damages or losses associated with the content in this product. While every attempt has been made to verify the information shared in this publication, neither the author nor the affiliates assume any responsibility for errors, omissions or contrary interpretation of the subject matter herein. Any perceived slights to any specific person(s) or organization(s) are purely unintentional. We have no control over the nature, content and availability of the web sites listed in this book.

The inclusion of any web site links does not necessarily imply a recommendation or endorse the views expressed within them. IMB Publishing takes no responsibility for, and will not be liable for, the websites being temporarily unavailable or being removed from the Internet.

The accuracy and completeness of information provided herein and opinions stated herein are not guaranteed or warranted to produce any particular results, and the advice and strategies, contained herein may not be suitable for every individual. The author shall not be liable for any loss incurred as a consequence of the use and application, directly or indirectly, of any information presented in this work. This publication is designed to provide information in regard to the subject matter covered.

The information included in this book has been compiled to give an overview of the subject and detail some of the symptoms, treatments etc. that are available. It is not intended to give medical advice. For a firm diagnosis of any health condition, and for a treatment plan suitable for you, you should consult your veterinarian or consultant.

The writer of this book and the publisher are not responsible for any damages or negative consequences following any of the treatments or methods highlighted in this book. Website links are for informational purposes and should not be seen as a personal endorsement; the same applies to the products detailed in this book. The reader should also be aware that although the web links included were correct at the time of writing, they may become out of date in the future.